交通运输职业教育高职汽车运用与维修技术专业教材

Qiche Zhuanye Yingyu

汽车专业英语

全国交通运输职业教育教学指导委员会　**组织编写**
　　　　　　　　　　　　　苏庆列　**主　编**
谢东梅　陈瑞娟　Alexander·JKM　**副 主 编**
　　　　　　　　　　　　　彭小红　**主　审**

人民交通出版社股份有限公司
China Communications Press Co.,Ltd.

内 容 提 要

本书为交通运输职业教育高职汽车运用与维修技术专业教材。本书分为8个模块,主要内容包括:汽车维修概述、汽车发动机、汽车底盘、汽车电控、汽车电器、汽车安全与舒适、新能源汽车、智能网联汽车。

本书可作为高等职业院校汽车运用与维修技术专业、汽车检测与维修技术专业的教学用书,也可作为汽车检测与维修技术人员的培训教材。

图书在版编目(CIP)数据

汽车专业英语/全国交通运输职业教育教学指导委员会组织编写;苏庆列主编.—北京:人民交通出版社股份有限公司,2019.8(2024.12重印)

ISBN 978-7-114-15615-1

Ⅰ.①汽… Ⅱ.①全… ②苏… Ⅲ.①汽车工程—英语—高等职业教育—教材 Ⅳ.①U46

中国版本图书馆 CIP 数据核字(2019)第 110523 号

书　　名	汽车专业英语
著 作 者	苏庆列
责任编辑	张一梅
责任校对	张　贺
责任印制	刘高彤
出版发行	人民交通出版社股份有限公司
地　　址	(100011)北京市朝阳区安定门外馆斜街3号
网　　址	http://www.ccpcl.com.cn
销售电话	(010)85285911
总 经 销	人民交通出版社股份有限公司发行部
经　　销	各地新华书店
印　　刷	北京虎彩文化传播有限公司
开　　本	787×1092　1/16
印　　张	11.5
字　　数	269千
版　　次	2019年8月　第1版
印　　次	2024年12月　第4次印刷
书　　号	ISBN 978-7-114-15615-1
定　　价	29.00元

(有印刷、装订质量问题的图书,由本公司负责调换)

前　言

为贯彻落实《国务院关于印发〈国家教育事业发展"十三五"规划〉的通知》（国发〔2017〕4号）精神，深化教育教学改革，提高汽车技术人才培养质量，满足创新型、应用型人才培养目标的需要，全国交通运输职业教育教学指导委员会组织来自全国交通职业院校的专业教师，按照教育部发布的《高等职业学校汽车运用与维修技术专业教学标准》的要求，紧密结合高职高专人才培养需求，编写了交通运输职业教育高职汽车运用与维修技术专业教材。

在本系列教材编写工作启动之初，全国交通运输职业教育教学指导委员会组织召开了交通运输职业教育高职汽车运用与维修技术专业教材编写大纲审定会，邀请行业内知名专家对该专业的课程体系和教材编写大纲进行了审定。教材初稿完成后，每种教材由一名资深专业教师进行主审，编写团队根据主审意见修改后定稿，实现了对书稿编写全过程的严格把关。

本系列教材在编写过程中，认真总结了全国交通职业院校的专业建设经验，注意吸收发达国家先进的职业教育理念和方法，形成了以下特色：

1. 与专业教学标准紧密衔接，立足先进的职业教育理念，注重理论与实践相结合，突出实践应用能力的培养，体现"工学结合"的人才培养理念，注重学生技能的提升。

2. 打破了传统教材的章节体例，采用模块式或单元+任务式编写体例，内容全面、条理清晰、通俗易懂，充分体现理实一体化教学理念。为了突出实用性和针对性，培养学生的实践技能，每个模块后附有技能实训；为了学习方便，每个模块后附有模块小结、思考与练习（每个单元后附有思考与练习）。

3. 在确定教材编写大纲时，充分考虑了课时对教学内容的限制，对教学内容进行优化整合，避免教学冗余。

4. 所有教材配有电子课件，大部分教材的知识点，以二维码链接动画或视频资源，做到教学内容专业化，教材形式立体化，教学形式信息化。

《汽车专业英语》是本系列教材之一。全书由福建船政交通职业学院苏庆列担任主编,谢东梅、陈瑞娟、Alexander·JKM担任副主编,陕西交通职业技术学院彭小红担任主审。参加本教材编写工作的有:梁霖锋(编写模块一),苏庆列(编写模块二、模块七、模块八),陈瑞娟(编写模块三),黄知秋(编写模块四),谢东梅(编写模块五),张光葳(编写模块六)。其中,谢东梅老师来自云南交通运输职业学院,Alexander·JKM来自肯尼亚马西奥亚职业技术学院,其他老师来自福建船政交通职业学院。

由于编者水平和经验有限,书中难免存在不足或疏漏之处,恳请广大读者提出宝贵意见,以便进一步修改和完善。

全国交通运输职业教育教学指导委员会
2019年2月

目 录

Module 1	**Overview of Vehicle Maintenance**	1
Part I	Reading Materials	1
Part II	Skill Training	13
Part III	Exercises	14
Part IV	Listening and Speaking	14
Module 2	**Engine**	17
Part I	Reading Materials	17
Part II	Skill Training	25
Part III	Exercises	27
Part IV	Listening and Speaking	27
Module 3	**Chassis**	29
Part I	Reading Materials	29
Part II	Skill Training	38
Part III	Exercises	39
Part IV	Listening and Speaking	40
Module 4	**Electronic Control System**	42
Part I	Reading Materials	42
Part II	Skill Training	48
Part III	Exercises	50
Part IV	Listening and Speaking	50
Module 5	**Automotive Electrical Equipment**	52
Part I	Reading Materials	52
Part II	Skill Training	60
Part III	Exercises	62
Part IV	Listening and Speaking	63
Module 6	**Safety and Comfort System**	65
Part I	Reading Materials	65
Part II	Skill Training	72
Part III	Exercises	75

	Part Ⅳ	Listening and Speaking	76
Module 7	**New Energy Vehicles**		**78**
	Part Ⅰ	Reading Materials	78
	Part Ⅱ	Skill Training	88
	Part Ⅲ	Exercises	89
	Part Ⅳ	Listening and Speaking	90
Module 8	**Smart Vehicle**		**92**
	Part Ⅰ	Reading Materials	92
	Part Ⅱ	Skill Training	102
	Part Ⅲ	Exercises	103
	Part Ⅳ	Listening and Speaking	104

附件1 参考译文 106
附件2 汽车专业词汇(检索 A-Z) 136
附件3 汽车维修手册缩略语表 168
参考文献 178

Module 1　Overview of Vehicle Maintenance

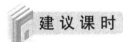

(1)能够用英语介绍轿车的类型；
(2)能够用英语介绍轿车的部件名称；
(3)能够用英语描述汽车的主要总成和作用；
(4)能够用英语介绍汽车维修的5S概念；
(5)能够用英语介绍汽车维修过程中的安全注意事项。

10课时。

Part Ⅰ　Reading Materials

Passage 1　Vehicle Categories

With the increasing popularity of automobiles in daily life, people's desire to know automobile related professional knowledge is also increasingly urgent. Let's first look at the car body parameters, as shown in Fig. 1-1.

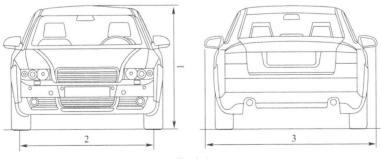

Fig. 1-1

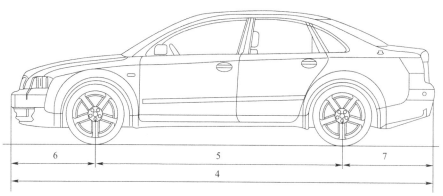

Fig. 1-1 Body size

1-Vehicle height /'viːɪkl haɪt/　　　　车高
2-Track /træk/　　　　　　　　　　　轮距
3-Vehicle width /wɪdθ/　　　　　　　车宽
4-Vehicle length /leŋθ/　　　　　　　 车长
5-Wheel base /wiːl beɪs/　　　　　　 轴距
6-Front overhang /frʌnt 'əʊvəhæŋ/　前悬
7-Rear /rɪə(r)/ overhang　　　　　　 后悬

Layouts

This section is a general introduction to the car as a whole. Over the years, many unusual designs have been tried, some with more success than others. The most common is, of course, a rectangular vehicle with a wheel at each corner! To take this rather simple idea further, we can categorize vehicles in different ways. For example, vehicles can be divided by layout (Fig. 1-2 to Fig. 1-5)such as:

(1)Front engine driving the front wheels;
(2)Front engine driving the rear wheels;
(3)Front engine driving all four wheels;
(4)Fear engine driving the rear wheels;

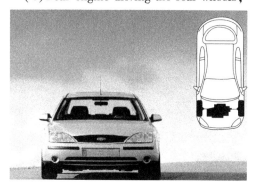

Fig. 1-2　Front-engine, front-wheel drive

Fig. 1-3　Front-engine, rear-wheel drive

 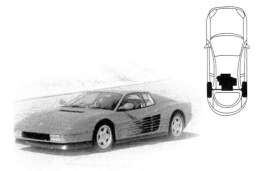

Fig. 1-4 Rear-engine, rear-wheel drive   Fig. 1-5 Mid-engine, rear-wheel drive

(5) Mid-engine driving the rear wheels;
(6) Mid-engine driving all four wheels.

The following paragraphs and bullet points highlight features of the vehicle layouts mentioned above. Common abbreviations for these layouts are given in Table 1-1.

Common abbreviations   Table 1-1

FWD	Front-wheel drive	AWD	All-wheel drive
RWD	Rear-wheel drive	4WD	Four-wheel drive

A common layout for a standard car is the front-engine, front-wheel drive vehicle. This is because a design with the engine at the front driving the front wheels has a number of advantages:

(1) It provides protection in the case of a front-end collision;
(2) Engine cooling is easier because of the air flow;
(3) Cornering can be better if the weight is at the front;
(4) Front-wheel drive adds further advantages if the engine is mounted sideways on (transversely);
(5) There is more room in the passenger compartment;
(6) The power unit can be made as a complete unit;
(7) The drive acts in the same direction as the steered wheels are pointing.

Rear-wheel driven by a front engine was the method used many years ago. Some manufacturers have continued its use, BMW for example. A long propeller shaft from the gearbox to the final drive, which is part of the rear axle, is the main feature. The propeller shaft has universal joints to allow suspension movement. This layout has some advantages:

(1) Weight transfers to the rear driving wheels when accelerating;
(2) Complicated constant universal joints, such as those used by front-wheel drive vehicles, are not needed.

Four-wheel drive combines all the advantages mentioned above but makes the vehicle more complicated and therefore is more expensive. The main difference of four-wheel drive is that an extra gearbox known as a transfer box is needed to link the front-wheel and rear-wheel drive.

The rear engine design has not been very popular but it was used for the best-selling car of all time: the VW Beetle. The advantages are that weight is placed on the rear wheels, giving good grip, and the power unit and drive can be all in one assembly. One downside is that less room is available for luggage in the front. The biggest problem is that handling is affected because of less weight on the steered wheels. Flat-type engines are the most common choice for this type of vehicle.

Fitting the engine in the mid-position of a car has one major disadvantage: it takes more space inside the vehicle. This makes it impractical for most "normal" vehicles. However, the distribution of weight is very good, which makes it the choice of high-performance vehicle designers. A good example is the Ferrari Testarossa. Mid-engine is the term used to describe any vehicle where the engine is between the axles, even if it is not in the middle.

Types

Types of light vehicle can range from small two-seat sports cars to large people carriers or sports utility vehicles (SUVs). Also included in the range are light commercial vehicles such as vans and pick-up trucks. It is hard to categorize a car exactly as there are several agreed systems in several different countries. Fig. 1-6 to Fig. 1-13 show a number of different body types.

Fig. 1-6　Saloon car(Source: Volvo Media)

Fig. 1-7　Estate car(Source: Ford Media)

Fig. 1-8　Hatchback(Source: Ford Media)

Fig. 1-9　Coupé(Source: Ford Media)

Fig. 1-10 Convertible(Source: Ford Media)

Fig. 1-11 Sports utility vehicle (SUV) (Source: Ford Media)

Fig. 1-12 Light van(Source: Ford Media)

Fig. 1-13 Pick-up truck (Source: Ford Media)

Passage 2 Main Systems

No matter how we categorize them, all vehicle designs have similar major components and these operate mostly in the same way. The four main areas of a vehicle are the vehicle body, engine, chassis and electrical systems. Its main components are shown in Fig. 1-14.

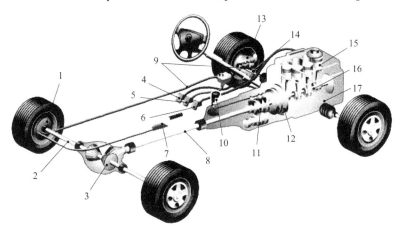

Fig. 1-14 Structure of vehicle

1-Brake /breIk/ (Drum Type)　　　　　　　　　制动器(鼓式)

2-Half shaft /hɑːf ʃɑːft/ 半轴
3-Final drive /ˈfainəl draiv/ 主减速器
4-Clutch pedal /klʌtʃ ˈpedl/ 离合器踏板
5-Brake pedal 制动踏板
6-Accelerator /əkˈseləreɪtə(r)/ 加速踏板
7-Handbrake /ˈhændbreɪk/ 驻车制动器
8-Propeller /prəˈpelə(r)/ shaft 传动轴
9-Brake pipes /paɪp/ 制动管
10-Gearstick /ˈɡɪəstɪk/ 变速器操纵杆
11-Gearbox /ˈɡɪəbɒks/ 变速器
12-Clutch 离合器
13-Brake (Disc Type) 制动器(盘式)
14-Steering arm /ˈstɪərɪŋ ɑːm/ 转向臂
15-Piston /ˈpɪstən/ 活塞
16-Crankshaft /ˈkræŋkʃɑːft/ 曲轴
17-Engine /ˈendʒɪn/ 发动机

Engine

Fig. 1-15 Ford Focus engine

This area consists of the engine itself together with fuel, ignition, air supply and exhaust systems (Fig. 1-15). In the engine, a fuel-air mixture enters through an inlet manifold and is fired in each cylinder in turn. The resulting expanding gases push on pistons and connecting rods which are on cranks, just like a cyclist's legs driving the pedals, and this makes a crankshaft rotate. The pulses of power from each piston are smoothed out by a heavy flywheel. Power leaves the engine through the flywheel, which is fitted on the end of the crankshaft, and passes to the clutch. The spent gases leave via the exhaust system.

Chassis

This area is made up of the braking, steering and suspension systems as well as the wheels and tires. Hydraulic pressure is used to activate the brakes to slow down or stop the vehicle. Rotating discs are gripped between pads of friction lining (Fig. 1-16). The hand brake uses a mechanical linkage to operate parking brakes. Both front wheels are linked mechanically and must turn together to provide steering control. The most common method is to use a rack and pinion. The steering wheel is linked to the pinion and as this is turned it moves the rack to and fro, which in turn moves the wheels. Tires also absorb some road shock and play a very important part in road holding. Most of the remaining shocks and vibrations are absorbed by springs in the driver and passenger seats. The springs can be coil type and are used in conjunction with a damper to stop the oscillating (bouncing up and down too much).

In this area, the clutch allows the driver to disconnect drive from the engine and move the vehicle off from rest. The engine flywheel and clutch cover are bolted together so that the clutch always rotates with the engine, and when the clutch pedal is raised, drive is passed to the gearbox. A gearbox is needed because an engine produces power only when turning quite quickly. The gearbox allows the driver to keep the engine at its best speed. When the gearbox is in neutral, power does not leave it. A final drive assembly and differential connect the drive to the wheels vial axles or drive-shafts (Fig. 1-17). The differential allows the drive-shafts and hence the wheels to rotate at different speeds when the vehicle is cornering.

Fig. 1-16 Disc brakes and part of the suspension system

Fig. 1-17 Differential and final drive components

Electrical

The electrical system covers many aspects such as lighting, wipers and instrumentation. A key component is the alternator (Fig. 1-18) which, driven by the engine, produces electricity to run the electrical systems and charge the battery. A starter motor takes energy from the battery to crank over and start the engine. Electrical components are controlled by a range of switches. Electronic systems use sensors to detect conditions and actuators to control a variety of things—in fact, on modern vehicles, almost everything.

Fig. 1-18 A modern alternator

Passage 3 5S Concept in Workshop

Operators need to comply with regulations regarding safe working practices in order to reduce to a minimum the hazards to health and safety associated with automobile maintenance. To skilled and experienced operators, this does not mean that any additional restrictions are imposed on their activities, but merely that they should carry out their tasks with constant regard for the health and safety of themselves and their fellow workers. We can start with clean and tidy work dress, as shown in Fig. 1-19.

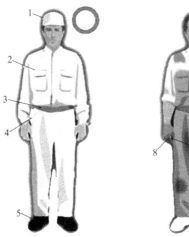

Fig. 1-19 Work dress

1- Safety hat /ˈseɪfti hæt/　　　　　安全帽
2- Work clothes /wəːk kləʊðz/　　　工作服
3- Belt without buckle /ˈbʌkl/　　　无扣的皮带
4- Pocket /ˈpɒkɪt/　　　　　　　　口袋
5- Safety shoes /ˈʃuːz/　　　　　　安全鞋
6- Key chain /kiː tʃein/　　　　　钥匙扣
7- Watch /wɒtʃ/　　　　　　　　手表
8- Ring /rɪŋ/　　　　　　　　　戒指
9- Key　　　　　　　　　　　钥匙
10- Dirty /ˈdɜːti/ hands　　　　　脏的手

5S concept

The 5S activity originated in Japan is an excellent on-site management technology. The 5S is the key to maintain the workshop and enable easy, fast and reliable (safe) operations.

How to ensure the quality of car maintenance?

(1) Keep the workplace tidy and orderly.

(2) Try to keep the workplace clean and tidy. First of all, don't pollute it.

SEIRI (Ordering)

Purpose: This process will determine whether a certain item is needed or not. Unnecessary items should be discarded immediately in order to make efficient use of space (Fig. 1-20).

(1) Organize and utilize all resources, including tools, parts, or information, as necessary.

(2) Assign a place on the work site to store all unnecessary items.

(3) Collect unnecessary items from the workplace and then discard them properly and legally.

(4) Discard unwanted items.

Fig. 1-20 Ordering

SEITON (Rectifying)

Purpose: To facilitate the use of parts and tools and to save time (Fig. 1-21).

(1) Keep seldom-used articles in a separate place.

(2) Put occasionally-used articles in your workplace.

(3) Put commonly-used articles on your side.

SEISO (Sweeping)

Purpose: Remove dirt from the workplace so that the equipment is always in a completely normal condition and can be used at any time (Fig. 1-22).

(1) A dirty work environment is a reflection of lack of confidence.

(2) Be sure to develop a good habit of keeping the workplace clean.

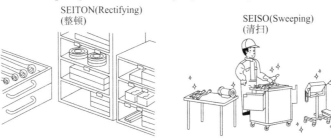

Fig. 1-21 Rectifying   Fig. 1-22 Sweeping

SEIKETSU (Cleaning)

Purpose: Cleaning is a process of trying to keep ordering, rectifying and cleaning up to prevent any possible problems (Fig. 1-23).

Fig. 1-23 Cleaning

(1) Everything shall serve the purpose of a clean environment, such as colors, shapes, layout of various articles, lighting, ventilation, display racks, and personal hygiene.

(2) If the work environment becomes fresh and bright, it can give the customer a good atmosphere.

SHITSUKE (Self-discipline)

Self-discipline is also known as literacy.

SHITSUKE(Self-discipline)
(自律)

Fig. 1-24 Self-discipline

Purpose: Self-discipline is a process for employees to develop awareness and habits through training and then become proud (Fig. 1-24).

(1) Self-discipline forms the cultural foundation, which is the most basic requirement for ensuring harmony with the society.

(2) Self-discipline is the training in the study of rules and regulations. Through such training, the trainees can learn to respect others and make others feel comfortable.

Passage 4 Safety Precautions

When working in the workshop, we need to use various tools, as shown in Figure 1-25. At the same time, special hazards may be encountered in the workshop.

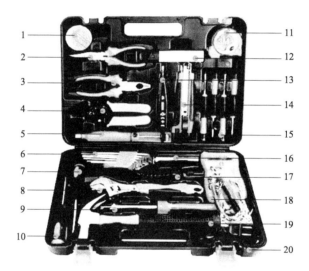

Fig. 1-25 Tool kit

1-Electrical tape /iˈlektrikəl teip/   电工胶布

2-Long nose pliers /lɔŋ nəuz ˈplaɪəz/   尖嘴钳

3-Vise /vaɪs/   老虎钳

4-Network clamp /klæmp/   网络钳

5-Suction pump /ˈsʌkʃən pʌmp/   吸锡泵

6-Allen wrench /rentʃ/   内六角扳手

7-Slotted screwdriver /ˈskru:draɪvə(r)/   一字螺丝刀

8-Adjustable /əˈdʒʌstəbl/ wrench   活动扳手

9-Tip electric iron /iˈlektrikˈaiən/   尖嘴电烙铁

10-Phillips screwdriver   十字螺丝刀

11-Tape measure /teip ˈmeʒə/   卷尺

12-Artist blade /bleɪd/ 美工刀片
13-Electrician /ɪˌlek'trɪʃn/ pen 电工笔
14-Utility /juː'tɪləti/ knife 美工刀
15-Screwdriver kit /kɪt/ 螺丝刀套件
16-Tin wire /tɪn 'waɪə/ 锡丝
17-Flashlight /'flæʃlaɪt/ 手电筒
18-Multimeter /'mʌltɪmiːtə/ 万用表
19-Hammer /'hæmə(r)/ 铁锤
20-Plastic /'plæstɪk/ box 塑料箱

The safety precautions are as follows:

(1) Do wash hands before eating, drinking or using toilet facilities to avoid transferring the residues of sealers, pigments, solvents, filings of steel, lead and other metals from the hands to the inner parts and other sensitive areas of the body.

(2) Do not use kerosene, thinners or solvents to wash the skin. They remove the skin's natural protective oils and can cause dryness and irritation or have serious toxic effects. Do not overuse waterless hand cleaners, soaps or detergents, as they can remove the skin's protective barrier oils. Always use barrier cream to protect the hands, especially against fuels, oils, greases, hydrocarbon solvents and solvent-based sealers. Do follow work practices that minimize the contact of exposed skin and the length of time that liquids or substances stay on the skin. Do thoroughly wash contaminants such as used engine oil from the skin as soon as possible with soap and water. A waterless hand cleaner can be used when soap and water are not available. Always apply skin cream after using waterless hand cleaner. Do not put contaminated or oily rags in pockets or tuck them under a belt, as this can cause continuous skin contact.

(3) Do not dispose of dangerous fluids by pouring them on the ground, or down drains or sewers.

(4) Do not continue to wear overalls which have become badly soiled or which have acid, oil, grease, fuel or toxic solvents spill over them. The effect of prolonged contact from heavily soiled overalls with the skin can be cumulative and life threatening. If the solvents are become flammable from the effect of body temperature, a spark from welding or grinding could envelop the wearer in flames with disastrous consequences. Do not clean dusty overalls with an air line: it is more likely to blow the dust into the skin, with possible serious or even fatal results. Do wash contaminated or oily clothing before wearing it again. Do discard contaminated shoes. Wear only shoes which afford adequate protection to the feet from the effect of dropping tools and sharp or heavy objects on them, and also from red hot and burning materials. Sharp or hot objects could easily penetrate unsuitable footwear such as canvas plimsolls or trainers. The soles of the shoes should also be maintained in good condition to guard against upward penetration by sharp or hot pieces of metal.

(5) Ensure gloves are free from holes and are clean on the inside. Always wear them when handling materials of a hazardous or toxic nature.

(6) Keep goggles clean and in good condition. Renew the glass or goggles as necessary. Never use goggles with cracked glasses. Always wear goggles when using a bench grindstone or portable grinders, disc sanders, power saws and chisels.

(7) Smoking can be allowed only in the smoking area. Smoking in the maintenance workplace is prohibited.

(8) A traveling car for normal use does not need to be constantly recharged, but if the car is often driven for a short distance or if not driven for a long time, the battery needs to be recharged. Disconnect the battery from the in-car electrical system when charging.

(9) If there is a great number of personnel on the site, be sure to organize the personnel and nearby vehicles to evacuate while extinguishing the fire. The time for self-rescue is generally within one minute. Remember to apply the fire extinguisher first of all. Proper processing within tens of seconds just after the fire started plays an extremely crucial role in changing danger of life and property into safety. If the fire becomes strong and it is estimated that it is burning out of control, the evacuation should be organized and the 119 professional fire brigade should be called.

(10) Electric shock can result from the use of faulty and poorly maintained electrical equipment or misuse of equipment. All electrical equipment must be frequently checked and maintained in good condition. Flexes, cables and plugs must not be frayed, cracked, cut or damaged in any way. Equipment must be protected by the correctly rated fuse. Use low-voltage equipment wherever possible.

(11) How to operate the grinding wheel:

①Do not wear gloves;

②Check for looseness before starting the grinding wheel;

③Do not stand in front of the grinding wheel;

④Do not start grinding until the wheel rotates steadily;

⑤Do not hit the grinding wheel;

⑥Clamping a small work piece (do not use ordinary pliers).

(12) How to operate a drilling machine:

①Wear goggles;

②Do not wear gloves (especially cotton gloves);

③Fix the drill (until it is concentric, not eccentric);

④Check for looseness before starting the grinding wheel;

⑤Fix the work piece (clamp a small work piece with flat pliers and the like);

⑥Select the feed speed (slow down when it is about to drill through);

⑦Clean the iron filings with a broom (instead of blowing off).

(13) Emergency treatment for iron filings getting in your eyes:

①Do not rub the eye by hand.

②Do not flush the eye with water.

③It is recommended to remove the iron filings from the eye carefully with soft paper.

④If necessary, call a doctor.

(14) How to use hand tools:

①For a wrench, generally, pull it instead of pushing. Be sure to push it carefully to avoid injuring the hand.

②For a hammer, check if it becomes loose. No burrs at the end of the hammer are allowed.

(15) Treatment of scald:

①If you get scalded, cool the scalded skin with cold water as usual. Be careful that water flow will break through the skin. It is recommended to apply special burn cream to the skin.

②If scalded, be sure to call a doctor as soon as possible.

Part Ⅱ Skill Training

Circuit Identification

Explain the contents indicated by 1 to 8 in the following Toyota circuit diagrams (Fig. 1-26).

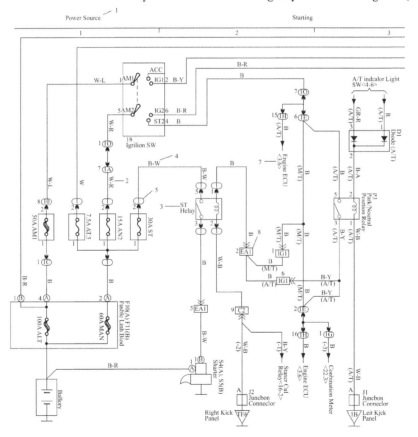

Fig. 1-26 Toyota circuit diagram

1-System name; 2-Wire color; 3-Component location; 4-Terminal number; 5-Relay box; 6-Junction box; 7-Associated system; 8-Connector.

Part Ⅲ Exercises

Text Review

Exercise 1: Translate the following phrases into Chinese or English.

1. _____   Front-engine, front-wheel drive
2. 承载式车身   _____
3. _____   SUV
4. 梯形车架   _____
5. _____   front bumper
6. 发动机舱盖   _____
7. _____   Differential
8. 电击   _____
9. _____   safety shoes
10. 护目镜   _____

Exercise 2: Mark the following statements with T (True) or F (False) according to the passage.

(   ) 1. The main difference with rear-wheel drive is that an extra gearbox known as a transfer box is needed to link the front-and rear-wheel drive.

(   ) 2. The 5S activity originated in Germany is an excellent on-site management technology.

(   ) 3. Wearing sandals or athletic shoes can also easily result in personal injuries due to accidentally falling objects.

(   ) 4. Electric shock can result from the use of faulty and poorly maintained electrical equipment or misuse of equipment.

(   ) 5. If scalded, be sure to call a doctor as soon as possible.

Exercise 3: Translate the following paragraph into Chinese.

In a word, a car can be divided into different categories according to different criteria. We need to understand the structure of the car, be familiar with the principle of the components, carry out comprehensive maintenance and repair of the car. When it comes to car maintenance, it's important to adhere to the 5S concept, and pay attention to the operation details of many equipment and tools.

Part Ⅳ Listening and Speaking

Buy a Car

Dialogue 1

A: Hello, sir! I am Li Ming. Here is my name card. What can I do for you today?

B: I am looking for a car.

A: You have come to the right place. We are the biggest dealer and we offer something big. What should I call you, sir?

B: Wong is my surname.

A: Thank you, Mr. Wong. Would you please take a seat here? Then we can talk over to find out the best car for you.

B: Thank you!

A: Here is our brochure, and you may browse through it. We are giving special offers to many types in it.

B: That's great.

A: Mr. Wong, what kind of car do you want?

B: We need a car with more room. My wife and I are about to have a baby.

A: Congratulations! Do you prefer some certain type?

B: I'd like to check out SUV.

A: May I ask how much is your budget?

B: About 250 thousand YUAN.

A: Not a problem sir. We have a nice brand new Audi Q3 SUV over here. It's of really tech-savvy. The sticker price is 250 thousand YUAN. It is just the one for you.

B: Any gifts?

A: Yes. You may get a set of seat covers or a set of floor mats for free. Which one do you prefer?

B: Both. May I have both?

A: OK. Both are yours. Hope you like what we offer and that you will love to recommend us.

B: Thank you. I will if the car is indeed nice.

Dialogue 2

A: How do you like this car, Mr. Wong? It is really nice and it just asks for $30,000.

B: Honda Pilot. I actually was looking for a Honda Pilot. I went online last night to check out the blue book value on new Pilots. The price I saw was $27,000. Why is your price higher?

A: Well sir, difference price goes with different features. At this car dealership we offer a free bumper to bumper warranty and we have very cheap extended warranties.

B: That's great, but every car dealership offers that. I'm not going to pay the sticker price for this car. I will pay the blue book value of $27,000.

A: I can't offer you that price. What about $29,000?

B: No. I'll pay $27,000 or I'll go somewhere else that charges a fair price. Don't you want my business?

A: We do want your business, sir. Let me talk to my manager and see what I can do. Give me five minutes.

A: Sir, I talked to my manager and he said that there are some factory to dealer incentives that I didn't know about. I can get the price down to ＄28,000. Would that work for you?

B: No. Are you not listening to me? I will pay the correct price, which is ＄27,000. What do you say? If the answer is no, I will get to another dealership before it gets too late.

A: OK. I will sell the car to you for that price. We would like to have your business.

B: Great. I'll take the car, but don't even attempt to rip me off on the financing plan. I did my research on that too. Let's get this over with.

A: Sure. Trust me. Will you pay with full payment or by installments?

Customer: Full.

B: Nice. Just a moment. I will work out a purchase scheme for you. Mr. Wong, you are going to take Pilot Model LX (1.5L) at ＄27,000. When added with ＄2,500 for purchase tax and ＄500 for licensing service, it is exactly ＄30,000.

A: Got it. Thank you!

B: Thank you! Now let's fill out the paperwork.

Module 2　Engine

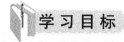

(1) 能够用英语介绍发动机曲柄连杆机构部件；
(2) 能够用英语描述发动机曲柄连杆机构的作用和工作原理；
(3) 能够用英语介绍发动机配气机构部件；
(4) 能够用英语描述发动机配气机构的作用和工作原理；
(5) 能够用英语介绍发动机润滑系统部件；
(6) 能够用英语描述发动机润滑系统的作用和工作原理；
(7) 能够用英语介绍发动机冷却系统部件；
(8) 能够用英语描述发动机电控系统电路图的组成和作用。

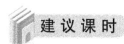

10 课时。

Part Ⅰ　Reading Materials

Passage 1　Crank-Link Mechanism

The crank and connecting rod mechanism is the main mechanism of a reciprocating engine for transforming thermal energy into mechanical energy. It transforms the reciprocating linear motion of the piston under action of pressure into the circular motion of the crankshaft to deliver power to the external components. See Fig. 2-1.

Crank and connecting rod mechanism consists of the piston and connecting rod group and the crankshaft and flywheel group. The piston and connecting rod group includes mainly the piston, piston rings, piston pin and connecting rod. The crankshaft and flywheel group includes mainly the crankshaft, flywheel, pulley and timing gear.

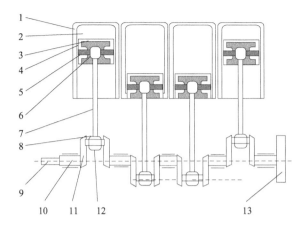

Fig. 2-1　Crank-link mechanism

1-Cylinder /ˈsɪlɪndə(r)/　　　　汽缸
2-Combustion chamber /tʃeimbə/　　燃烧室
3-Piston /ˈpɪstən/　　　　活塞
4-Piston ring　　　　活塞环
5-Piston pin /pɪn/　　　　活塞销
6-Small end　　　　连杆小头
7-Connecting rod /kəˈnektɪŋ rɔd/　　连杆
8-Big end　　　　连杆大头
9-Crankshaft　　　　曲轴
10-Main journal /mein ˈdʒəːnl/　　主轴颈
11-Crankweb /kˈræŋkweb/　　曲柄
12-Rod journal　　　　连杆轴颈
13-Flange plate /flændʒ pleit/　　凸缘盘

　　When the engine is running, the pressure of gases produced from fuel burning is directly appliedto the piston crown. The piston is hence driven to reciprocate along a straight line. The power applied by the piston is delivered via the piston pin and the connecting rod to the crankshaft. The reciprocating linear motion of the piston is transformed into the circular motion of the crankshaft. Large portion of the power produced by the engine is delivered to the driveline via the flywheel installed at the rear end of the crankshaft. The power is then delivered to the drive wheels of the vehicle, via the driveline. Another portion of the power produced by the engine is used to drive the accessories of the engine itself and other systems, via the gear and the pulley installed at the front end of the crankshaft.

Piston

　　The function of piston is to jointly constitute a combustion chamber with cylinder head and bear gas pressure, and to deliver the pressure to connecting rod through piston pin to drive rotation of crankshaft.

The piston can be divided into 3 parts, namely top, head and skirt by the structure. The piston crown is a component of combustion chamber and used to bear gas pressure. Shape of top of piston of gasoline engine is related to shape of the combustion chamber and compression ratio. The head of piston refers to the part above piston ring groove, and its functions are: to bear gas pressure and deliver it to connecting rod; to help to realize sealing of cylinder with piston ring; and to conduct the heat absorbed from top of piston to cylinder wall through piston ring. Skirt part of piston refers to the part below lower end of oil ring groove, and is used to provide orientation for piston motion and bear lateral pressure. Therefore, the skirt part shall have certain length to ensure reliable orientation; besides, it shall have sufficient actual pressure bearing area to bear lateral pressure.

Piston Ring

Piston ring is an elastic split ring, and can be divided into gaseous ring and oil ring based on its' function.

The gaseous ring, also called compression ring, is used to ensure sealing between piston and cylinder wall and avoid gas in cylinder moving to crankcase; deliver the heat on the head of piston to cylinder wall, then take it away through cooling water or air; in addition, it plays a subsidiary role in scraping and distributing oil. There are 2-3 gaseous rings being equipped in each piston on engine generally.

Oil ring is used to scrape away redundant engine oil on the cylinder wall, and paints a layer of well-distributed oil film on the cylinder wall, which can not only avoid that engine oil jumps into the cylinder and burns, but also reduce the abrasion and frictional resistance among piston, piston ring and cylinder. Moreover, the oil ring plays a subsidiary role in sealing. In general, there are 1-2 oil rings on engine.

Piston Pin

The function of piston pin is to connect piston and small end of connecting rod, and deliver the gas pressure borne by piston to connecting rod.

The piston pin undertakes very large periodic impact load under high temperature, and has poor lubrication condition (generally depending on splash lubrication), which thus requires that the piston pin has sufficient stiffness and strength, wear-proof surface and small mass as far as possible. To this end, the piston pin is usually made to be a hollow cylinder.

Connecting Rod

The function of the connecting rod is to pass the force on the piston to the crankshaft and push the crankshaft to turn, so that the reciprocating motion of the piston is transformed into the rotating motion of the crankshaft.

The connecting rod is under alternating load such as compression, stretching and bending at work. Therefore, it is required that the connecting rod should be as small as possible with sufficient stiffness and strength.

Crankshaft

The main function of the crankshaft is to bear the force transmitted by the connecting rod, and thus produce the rotating torque around the axis of its own, which is exported through the flywheel. In addition, the crankshaft is also used to drive the engine's valve train and generators, pumps, steering oil pumps, air compressors and other accessories.

The crankshaft is usually made up of the front end, the main journal, the connecting rod journal (crank pin), the crank arm, the counterweight and the rear end (the power output end) and so on. The crankshaft front axle is used to install the pump pulley, the crankshaft timing pulley (or the timing gear, the timing sprocket), the starting paw and so on. The rear flange of the crankshaft is used to install the flywheel.

Flywheel

A flywheel is a disk with large moment of inertia, and its main function is to ensure the rotation speed and the output torque of the crankshaft as uniform as possible, to make the engine run smoothly and to overcome a short time overload. In addition, it is often used as a flywheel friction type clutch driving member. At the same time, the force is transferred when the gear ring on the flywheel starts.

Passage 2 Valve Mechanism

The valve mechanism closes and opens the intake valves and exhaust valves according to the firing order of the cylinders, so that fresh air-fuel mixture (in the case of a gasoline engine) or air (in the case of a diesel engine) can timely enter the cylinders, and waste gases resulting from combustion can timely go out of the cylinders.

The valve mechanism consists of the valve group and the valve train group. The valve group includes mainly the valves (intake valves and exhaust valves), valve springs, valve seats, and valve guides. The valve train group include mainly the camshafts, timing pulleys (or gear, or sprocket), timing belt (or timing chain) and valve tappets. See Fig. 2-2.

The timing pulleys of the camshafts are driven by the timing pulley of the crankshaft, via the timing belt. The valve sub-assemblies are driven, via the valve tappets, by the timing pulleys of the camshafts. Due to the special profile and arrangement of the cams on the camshafts, the intake and exhaust valves are opened and closed accurately in good time, with the gas change of the cylinders accomplished.

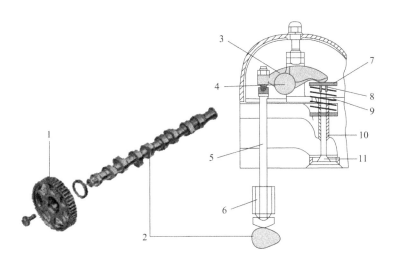

Fig. 2-2 Valve mechanism

1-Camshaft /ˈkæmʃɑːft/ timing gear /gɪə/   凸轮轴正时齿轮
2-Camshaft   凸轮轴
3-Rocker arm /ˈrɔkə ɑːm/   摇臂
4-Rockshaft /ˈrɒkʃɑːft/   摇臂轴
5-Valve lifter /vælv ˈlɪftə/ / push rod   推杆
6-Valve tappet /ˈtæpɪt/   挺柱
7-Valve spring seat   气门弹簧座
8-Valve keys / collets /kɒˈlɪts/   气门锁片
9-Valve spring   气门弹簧
10-Valve pipe / valve guide /gaɪd/   气门导管
11-Valve   气门

Valve

The valves on the cylinder head are used to open or to close the intake and exhaust ports of each cylinder. The valve at the intake port is called the intake valve, and the one at the exhaust port is called the exhaust valve.

The operating conditions of the valves are very hard. First, each valve directly contacts with high-temperature gas. It is exposed to heat which is difficult to be dispersed. As a result, its operating temperature is high. Compared to exhaust valve temperature up to 600-800℃, intake valve temperature can also reach 300-400℃. Second, the valve is subjected to gas force, valve spring force and inertia moment impact from valve seat. Third, the valve is cooled and lubricated poorly. Therefore, the valve is required to have sufficient strength and rigidity, and should be resistant to heat, wear and corrosion.

Valve Seat

The position where the cylinder head engages with the valve cone face is called the valve seat. The valve seat, together with the valve head, acts as a seal against the cylinder and at the same time receives the heat from the valve head and acts as a heat sink for the valve.

The valve seat is easy to be worn because it suffers from high temperature, high-frequency impact of valve head, and poor lubrication. Therefore, aluminum cylinder heads and most cast iron cylinder heads are designed with inlaid valve retainers made of materials that are resistant to high temperature and wear.

Valve Guide

The valve guide is a seat hole for supporting the valve in the cylinder head, and its function is to guide the movement of the valve to ensure that the valve reciprocates linearly, so that the valve fits the valve seat correctly. In addition, it also acts as a heat conductor between the valve stem and the cylinder head.

Generally, there is a gap of 0.05-0.12 mm between the valve stem and the valve guide so that the valve stem can move freely in the valve guide pipe.

Valve Spring

The valve spring allows the valve to return and close automatically to ensure that the valve is in close contact with the valve seat and that the valve tappet contacts the cam surface without disengaging from each other.

The valve spring is generally a cylindrical coil spring with constant pitch. The lower end of the valve spring is supported in the spring retainer of the cylinder head and the upper end is pressed against the valve spring retainer on the valve stem.

Passage 3   Lubrication System

Function of Lubrication System

When the engine works, many parts move relatively with other parts in a small room, such as the main journal of the crankshaft and the main bearing; the rod journal and the rod bearing; piston, piston ring and cylinder wall; the camshaft and camshaft bearing etc. If the surfaces of these parts are not lubricated, severe friction happens and expedites the parts wear and finally makes it impossible for the engine to run. So the lubrication system is important to guarantee a long operation of the engine.

The function of the lubrication system is to continuously deliver adequate clean oil in right temperature to the friction surfaces of all moving parts, and to form the oil film between the friction surfaces for liquid friction, so as to reduce the friction resistance, power consumption and parts wear to improve the engine's reliability and durability. It also helps cooling and cleaning of engine parts as the oil circulates.

The Lubrication System of Gasoline Engine

The lubrication system of gasoline engine is normally composed of oil pump, suction filter, filter cleaner, pressure-limiting valve, by-pass valve and oil pipeline etc., and some have oil cooler too. See Fig. 2-3.

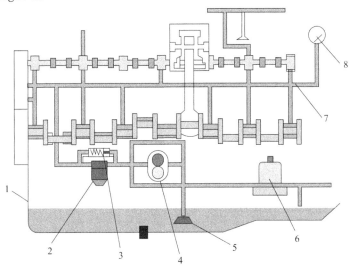

Fig. 2-3 Lubrication system

1-Oil pan /ɔil pæn/ 油底壳
2-Secondary oil filter /ˈsɛkənˌdɛri ɔɪl ˈfɪltɚ/ 机油粗滤器
3-Bypass /ˈbaɪpɑːs/ valve 旁通阀
4-Oil pump /pʌmp/ 机油泵
5-Suction /ˈsʌkʃn/ filter 集滤器
6-Primary /ˈpraɪməri/ oil filter 机油细滤器
7-Main oil gallery /ˈɡæləri/ 主油道
8-Oil pressure gauge /ˈprɛʃə ɡeɪdʒ/ 机油压力表

When the engine runs, the oil pump sucks in the engine oil from the oil pan through the suction filter which prevents the entry of big mechanical impurities into the oil pump and lubricating circuit. The engine oil pumped out flows through the filter cleaner into the main oil passage of the cylinder and then through the transverse oil passage in the crankcase into the main journal of the crankshaft. Then it flows from the main journal, passes through the slanting oil passage in the crankshaft, and then enters the rod journal where a little portion of the engine oil sprays to the piston and cylinder wall to lubricate them through the orifice on the big end of the rod. And some of the engine oil flows to the oil passage on the cylinder cover through the oil passage on the cylinder body and then enters the camshaft bearing to lubricate the journal of the camshaft bearing. Furthermore, the lubricating oil also flows through relevant oil passage or orifice to the timing chain and its automatic tensioner (when the engine with time chain distribution mechanism is used), cam surface of the camshaft, hydraulic tappet (when the engine with hydraulic tappet is used) and so on to lubricate or work as the service fluid for the hydraulic parts.

Passage 4 Cooling system

Function of the Cooling System

The function of the cooling system is to make the engine get normal working temperature as quickly as possible and stay at the best working temperature in the whole working process.

The engine should be cooled down to the right extent. With under cooling, the engine is overheated to lead to the decrease of the intake efficiency and a higher tendency of resignation and conflagration, which causes the engine power reduction. Overheated engine also reduces the clearance between the moving parts of the engine, making the parts unable to move normally or even stuck or broken. What's more, overheating also decreases the lubricating oil viscosity and makes the oil film break easily, intensifying the parts wear. And also fuel consumption increases due to premature combustion.

With over cooling, the engine is too cold and the mixed gas or the air entering the cylinder has a too low temperature and is hard to ignite, leading to the reduction of the engine power and the increase of the oil consumption. The lubricating oil has a higher viscosity too, weakening the lubrication and increasing the parts wear. Furthermore, the fuel oil, which is not classifier yet due to the low temperature, shall wash against the oil film on the friction surfaces of the cylinder and piston etc. And as the mixed gas contacts the cooler cylinder wall, the classifier fuel oil shall condense again and flow into the crankcase, which shall not only increase the oil consumption but also make the oil thin and affect the lubrication, decreasing the engine power and intensifying the parts wear.

Water-Cooled Cooling System

The water-cooled cooling system uses water (or cooling liquid) as the coolant. The heat from the heated engine parts is transferred to the coolant first and then dissipates to the air through the radiator. The engine adopting the water-cooled cooling system is also called water-cooled engine. Its cooling system includes radiator, water pump, fan, cooling water jacket and thermostat etc (Fig. 2-4). Water pump is used in this system to force the coolant to circulate in the system to dissipate the heat.

Module 2 Engine

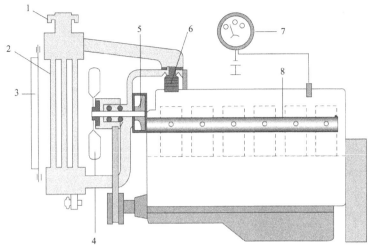

Fig. 2-4 Cooling system

1-Radiator cap /ˈreɪdiːˌeɪtə kæp/   散热器盖
2-Radiator   散热器
3-Shutter /ˈʃʌtə(r)/   百叶窗
4-Cooling fan /ˈkuːlɪŋ fæn/   冷却风扇
5-Water pump   水泵
6-Thermostat /ˈθɜːməstæt/   节温器
7-Water temperature /ˈtemprətʃə(r)/ meter   水温表
8-Water jacket /ˈdʒækɪt/   水套

Both the cylinder cover and the cylinder body of the water-cooled engine have inside the castled water jacket mutually connected. With the pump function, the cooling water in the radiator is pressed and flows through the inlet on the cylinder body into the engine, and then through the water jacket in the cylinder body and cover to absorb heat and returns afterwards from the outlet on the cylinder cover to the radiator along the water channel. Due to the auto speed and the powerful suction by the fan, the air passes through the radiator at a high speed from the front to the rear. So, when the heated cooling water flows through the radiator core, heat dissipates constantly into the air. The cooled water flows to the radiator bottom and then is pumped out and pressed into the water jacket of the engine and cycles repeatedly in this way. The heat is continuously transported to the air to cool down the engine and to guarantee the normal operation of the engine.

Part II Skill Training

Circuit Identification

Read the circuit diagram (Fig. 2-5) of VIOS's engine ECU and answer the following two questions.

(1) What are the main functions of ECU?

(2) What are the main sensors and actuators of the circuit diagram of VIOS?

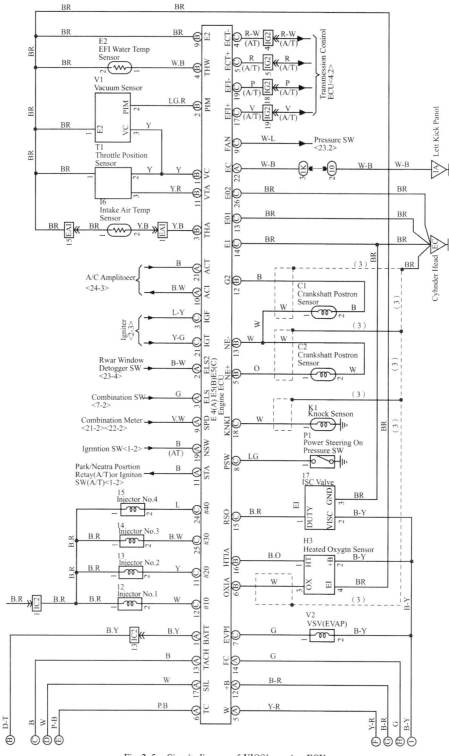

Fig. 2-5 Circuit diagram of VIOS's engine ECU

Part III Exercises

Text Review

Exercise 1: Translate the following phrases into Chinese or English.

1. _____   crankshaft
2. 凸轮轴   _____
3. _____   cylinder
4. 活塞环   _____
5. _____   journal
6. 连杆   _____
7. _____   valve seat
8. 润滑系统   _____
9. _____   thermostat
10. 飞轮   _____

Exercise 2: Mark the following statements with T (True) or F (False) according to the passage.

(   ) 1. According to the passage crank and connecting rod mechanism consists of the piston and connecting rod group and the crankshaft and flywheel group.

(   ) 2. The valves on the cylinder head are used to open the intake and exhaust ports of each cylinder.

(   ) 3. Lubrication system can continuously deliver adequate clean fuel in right temperature to the friction surfaces of all moving parts.

(   ) 4. When the heated cooling water flows through the radiator core, heat dissipates constantly into the air.

(   ) 5. Generally, an automotive engine consists of two mechanisms and five systems.

Exercise 3: Translate the following paragraph into Chinese.

Generally, an automotive engine consists of the following mechanisms and systems: engine body, crank and connecting rod mechanism, valve mechanism, lubrication system, cooling system, fuel system, ignition system and starting system. Furthermore, a modern engine is equipped with the emission control unit, and a supercharged engine is equipped with the supercharging system.

Part IV   Listening and Speaking

Purchase Insurance

Dialogue 1

A: What kind of car insurance do you have?

B: I went with the PICC.

A: Why did you choose that company?

B: I compared the price of the type of insurance that I wanted.

A: What should I think about in choosing services?

B: There are websites on which you will figure out what coverage is right for you.

A: What did you end up buying?

B: Well, my car is very old, so I didn't worry so much about what it would cost to repair it. I did buy a lot of coverage for fixing someone else's car.

A: Have you ever had to use your insurance?

B: No. I was in an accident, but it was the other person's fault and their insurance covered it.

Dialogue 2

A: Hello, I would like to learn about car insurance prices.

B: Sure. Please have a seat.

A: Thank you. I've just bought a new car.

B: Great, congratulations! What kind of car is it?

A: It's a Honda Pilot.

B: Oh, it's nice.

A: Yes, it is appealing to me. So, how much would the payment be?

B: It depends. Have you ever been in any accidents?

A: No, I have not.

B: Have you got any driving tickets?

A: Nope. Does that affect the insurance rate?

B: At times. Well, everything seems in order. You would have to pay $650 for one year.

A: That sounds great.

Module 3　Chassis

(1) 能够用英语介绍离合器的部件；
(2) 能够用英语描述离合器的作用和工作原理；
(3) 能够用英语介绍自动变速器的部件；
(4) 能够用英语描述自动变速器的作用和工作原理；
(5) 能够用英语介绍行驶系统的部件；
(6) 能够用英语描述行驶系统各部件的作用和工作原理；
(7) 能够用英语介绍制动系统的部件；
(8) 能够用英语描述制动系统各部件的作用和工作原理。

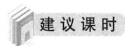

10 课时。

Part Ⅰ　Reading Materials

Passage 1　Clutch

　　The clutch is an integral part of the driveline. It is usually mounted at the rear end of the crankshaft and the flywheel of the engine to disengage or engage power transmission between the engine and the MT.

Functions of Clutch

(1) Gradually engaging the engine and driveline to ensure a smooth start of the vehicle.
(2) Interrupting power transmission and assisting in gear-shifting to make smooth shifting.
(3) Preventing the driveline from overloading.
(4) Providing a temporary neutral gear.

Basic Composition of Clutch

　　The clutch consists of drive components, driven components, a pressing device and a release mechanism. See Fig. 3-1.

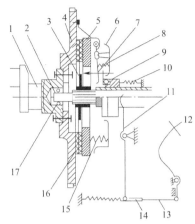

Fig. 3-1 Clutch

1-Crankshaft /ˈkræŋkʃɑːft/	曲轴
2-Driven shaft /ˈdrɪvən ʃɑːft/	从动轴
3-Driven plate /ˈdrɪvən pleɪt/	从动盘
4-Flywheel /ˈflaɪwiːl/	飞轮
5-Pressure plate /ˈpreʃə pleɪt/	压盘
6-Cover /ˈkʌvə(r)/	盖
7-Release lever /rɪˈliːs ˈliːvə(r)/	分离杠杆
8-Spring /sprɪŋ/	弹簧
9-Release bearing /rɪˈliːs ˈbɛərɪŋ/	分离轴承
10-Offsetting spring /ˈɔːfˌsetɪŋ sprɪŋ/	复位弹簧
11-Release yoke /jəʊk/	分离叉
12-Pedal /ˈpedl/	踏板
13-Pull rod	拉杆
14-Adjusting fork	调节叉
15-Retainer spring /rɪˈteɪnə sprɪŋ/	压紧弹簧
16-Driven disc friction lining	从动盘摩擦片
17-Bearing /ˈbɛərɪŋ/	轴承

Drive Components

Drive components consist of the flywheel, the clutch cover, the pressure plate and others. They are connected with the engine crankshaft. The clutch cover is bolted to the flywheel. The torque is transmitted between the pressure plate and the clutch cover by 3-4 driven plates.

Driven Plate

The driven part of the clutch is the driven plate, also called clutch friction disk. When the clutch is normally engaged, the friction linings on both sides of the driven plate come into contact with the flywheel and the pressure plate respectively. The torque of the engine is transmitted to the driven plate by the friction between the contact surfaces of the flywheel, the pressure plate and the driven plate.

Diaphragm Spring

The pressing device is composed of several coil pressure springs or a diaphragm spring uniformly arranged along the circumference, which are installed between the pressure plate and the clutch cover to press the pressure plate and the driven plate tightly against the flywheel.

Release Mechanism

The release mechanism includes a clutch pedal, a transmission mechanism, a fork, a bearing sleeve, a bearing, a lever, a return spring and others.

Working Principle of Clutch

1. Clutch Engagement

If the clutch is engaged, the pressure spring presses tightly the flywheel, the driven plate and the pressure plate together. The torque of the engine is transmitted to the driven plate through the friction surfaces of the driven plate through the flywheel and the pressure plate, and to the input shaft of the transmission by the spline hub in the middle of the driven plate. The maximum torque that the clutch can transmit depends on the contact pressure and coefficient of friction between the friction surfaces, as well as the number and size of the friction surfaces.

2. Clutch Release Process

Depressing the clutch pedal disengages the clutch. Both the release sleeve and the release bearing are driven by the release fork to eliminate the gap between the release bearing and the release lever, and then the inner end of the release lever is moved forward until its outer end drives the pressure plate to overcome the spring force to move backward. At this moment, the driven plate uncouples the flywheel, so that the friction torque disappears, thus the power transmission is interrupted.

Passage 2 Automatic Transmission

An automatic transmission is a type of motor vehicle transmission that can automatically change gear ratios as the vehicle moves, and eliminates drivers fatigue of shifting gears manually. Like other transmission systems on vehicles, it allows an internal combustion engine, best suited to run at a relatively high rotational speed, to provide a range of speed and torque outputs necessary for vehicular travel.

The most popular form found in automobiles is the hydraulic automatic transmission. This system uses a fluid coupling in place of a friction clutch, and accomplishes gear changes by hydraulically locking and unlocking a system of planetary gears. The main components of the automatic transmission are shown in Fig. 3-2. Some machines with limited speed ranges or fixed engine speeds, only use a torque converter to provide a variable gearing of the engine to the wheels.

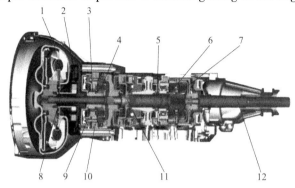

Fig. 3-2 Transmission

1-Hydraulic converter /haɪˈdrɔːlɪk kənˈvəːtə/   液力变矩器
2-Oil pump /ɔil pʌmp/   油泵
3-One-way clutch F_0 /ˈwʌnˈweɪ klʌtʃ/   单向离合器 F_0
4-Overdrive Planet Gearset /ˈgɪəset/   超速行星齿轮排
5-One-way clutch F_1 单向离合器 F_1
6-Front Planet Gearset   前行星齿轮排
7-Rear Planet Gearset   后行星齿轮排
8-Input shaft /ˈinput ʃɑːft/   输入轴
9-Clutch C_0 /klʌtʃ/   离合器 C_0
10-Brake B_0 /breɪk/   制动器 B_0
11-Intermediate /ˌɪntəˈmiːdjət/ shaft   中间轴
12-Output /ˈautput/ shaft   输出轴

The automatic transmission (AT) is used for the control of the clutch and the automation of speed shifting in automobile driving. At present, the automatic shifting process of the automatic transmission is controlled by the electronic control unit (ECU) of the automatic transmission.

Hydraulic Torque Converter

A torque converter is made of three parts: The impeller is located at the transmission end, attached to the housing, and is driven by the engine. The turbine is located at the engine side and is driven by the fluid flow from the impeller and drives the input shaft of the transmission. The stator redirects the flow to improve efficiency and multiply torque.

ATF Pump

As the ATF pump rotates, a low pressure (vacuum) is created as the pumping members move apart in one area, and atmospheric pressure will force fluid into this area. Pressure is created where the pumping members move together.

Planetary Gear Train

Consisting of planetary gear sets as well as friction clutches and brake bands. These are the mechanical systems that provide the various gear ratios, altering the speed of rotation of the output shaft depending on which planetary gears are locked.

To effect gear changes, one of two types of clutches or bands are used to hold a particular member of the planetary gear set motionless, while allowing another member to rotate, thereby transmitting torque and producing gear reductions or overdrive ratios. These clutches are actuated by the valve body (see below), their sequence controlled by the transmission's internal programming.

Hydraulic Control Valve Body

This control solenoid assembly contains four transmission fluid pressure (TFP) switches, a line pressure control solenoid, four pressure control (PC) solenoids, two shift solenoids (SS), a torque converter clutch (TCC) solenoid, a transmission fluid temperature (TFT) sensor and the transmission control module (TCM). It also has a vehicle harness connector, which connects to the shift position switch and the input and output speed sensors.

Electronic Control System

Automatic transmission inputs parameters such as the engine speed, throttle position, vehicle speed, engine water temperature, ATF oil temperature to the ECU through a variety of sensors. ECU analyzes, calculates and processes based on these signals, and then in accordance with the set shift law, issues action control signals to the shift solenoid valve, oil pressure solenoid valve. Shift solenoid valve and oil pressure solenoid valve then manipulate the ECU action control signals into hydraulic control signals to control the action of the various shift actuators in the valve plate, and thus achieve automatic shifting process.

Speed Sensors

Speed sensors are used by the powertrain control module (PCM) or the transmission control module (TCM) to control shifts and detect faults such as slippage when the two speeds do not match the predetermined ratio for each gear commanded.

Shift Lever

The shift control mechanism of the automatic transmission is a manual selection valve operating mechanism. The driver changes the position of the manual valve in the valve plate through the handle of the automatic transmission. The control system uses the automatic hydraulic control principle or the electronic automatic control principle according to the position of the manual valve, the throttle position, the vehicle speed, and the state of the control switch to control the operation of gear shifting actuator in the gear transmission according to certain laws, so as to achieve automatic gear shifting.

Passage 3 Running System

The driving system consists of the body (compartment), suspensions (front suspension, rear suspension), axles (steering driven axle, driving axle), wheels (steering wheels, driving wheels) and other assemblies. See Fig. 3-3.

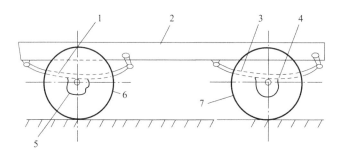

Fig. 3-3 Running system

1-Front suspension /sə'spenʃn/   前悬架
2-Frame /freɪm/   车架
3-Rear suspension   后悬架
4-Driving axle /'draɪvɪŋ 'æksəl/   驱动桥
5-Driven axle   从动桥
6-Front wheel   前轮
7-Rear wheel   后轮

The running system is used to integrate various assemblies and components of the vehicle into one body to support the entire vehicle and ensure driving.

Body

Modern cars apply integral body, which takes the vehicle body as the frame as well, and all parts and assemblies of the automobile are installed on the vehicle body, and the vehicle body shall bear functions of various loads. Therefore, such vehicle body becomes an integral body, which is widely used in cars and passenger cars.

Suspension

Although modern automobile suspensions have different structural forms, they are generally constituted by elastic components, shock absorber and stabilizer anti-roll bar, etc.

1. Elastic Components

Common elastic components in the automobile suspension are leaf spring, coil spring, torsion bar spring and hydro-gas spring, etc.

2. Shock Absorber

The shock absorber is used for reducing vibration of the vehicle body, attenuating the vibration amplitude rapidly, and maintaining contact between the wheels and the ground, so as to improve the ride comfort and handling stability of the automobile. At present, the automobiles make an extensive use of hydraulic shock absorber. When the frame and the axles make reciprocating relative motions, the oil liquid in the shock absorber flows through the valve opening on the piston repeatedly, thus the throttling action of the valve opening and the internal friction among the oil liquid molecules form the damping force for attenuating the vibration, which changes the vibration energy into heat energy to be absorbed by the oil liquid and the shock absorber' housing, and then be dissipated into the air.

3. Stabilizer Anti-roll Bar

The function of the stabilizer anti-roll bar is to improve the roll stiffness, make the automobile equipped with under-steer characteristic, and improve the handling stability and driving smoothness of the automobile. When the suspensions on both sides are of unequal deformations, the vehicle body runs off the straight against the road surface, and at this time, the twisting moment of the stabilizer bar plays the function of hindering deformation of the suspension spring, thus reducing the vehicle body's suspension roll and lateral angular vibrations.

Vehicle Axle

The axles are connected via the suspension and the frame (or integral body), with both ends installed with the automobile wheels, and its function is to transmit acting forces of various directions between the frame (or integral body) and the wheels as well as the bending moment and torque produced.

Wheel

The wheels are used for installing the tires, and bearing various load actions between the tires and the axles.

The wheels are constituted by the hubs, rims and spokes. The hubs are installed on the axles or on the knuckle's shaft diameter through conical roller bearing. The rims are used for installing and fixing the tires. The spokes are used for connecting the hubs and the rims.

In order to ensure running safety of the automobile, the wheel assembly of automobiles of high speed such as cars, passenger cars, etc. must be used only after dynamic wheel balancing measurement and adjustment, and the rim edges of such wheels are always clipped with counterbalance weights if necessary.

Spoke-type wheels are constituted by the rims, filter blocks, bolts, spokes and hubs, etc.

Passage 4　Braking System

Parking Brake System

The parking brake system (Fig. 3-4) is composed of hand brake lever, drive device and parking brake. It is controlled mechanically. When the brake is applied, the hand brake lever is pulled by the driver through the cable to allow the parking brake to function. Parking brake can be activated together with service brake. The control device uses the parking brake cable and the parking brake control device in the rear wheel brake to apply the rear wheel brake, which acts as a parking brake.

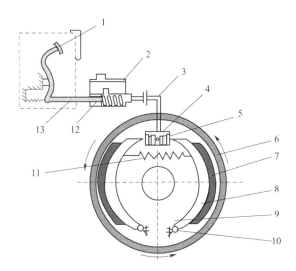

Fig. 3-4　Braking system

1-Brake pedal /breik 'pedl/　　　　　　　　　制动踏板
2-Brake master cylinder /breik 'mɑːstə 'silində/　　制动主缸
3-Oil tube /ɔil tjuːb/　　　　　　　　　　　　油管
4-Wheel braking cylinder /hwiːl' breikiŋ 'silində/　制动轮缸
5-Wheel cylinder piston /'pɪstən/　　　　　　　轮缸活塞
6-Brake drum /breik drʌm/　　　　　　　　　制动鼓
7-Friction /'frikʃən/ disk　　　　　　　　　　摩擦片
8-Brake shoe /breik ʃuː/　　　　　　　　　　制动蹄
9-Brake bottom /'bɑtəm/ plate　　　　　　　　制动底板
10-Supporting pin　　　　　　　　　　　　　支撑销
11-Brake shoe reset spring　　　　　　　　　　制动蹄复位弹簧
12-Brake master cylinder piston　　　　　　　　制动主缸活塞
13-Push rod /puʃ rɔd/　　　　　　　　　　　推杆

Drum Brake

The basic composition of the service brake system is shown under this paragraph (Fig 3-5). The rotating part of the wheel brake is the brake drum (8), which is fixed on the hub and connected with the wheel and rotates together with the wheel. The fixed part is the brake shoe (10) and the brake base plate (11) on which there are two support pins (12) supporting the lower ends of the two arc-shaped brake shoes (10). A friction plate (9) is riveted on the outer surface of the brake shoe, and the upper end is tightened against the piston (7) in the wheel cylinder (6) with a return spring (13). Both the support pins and the wheel cylinder are fixed on the brake base plate, and the brake base plate is bolted to the knuckle flange (front axle) or the axle housing flange (rear axle). The wheel cylinder (6) is connected to the hydraulic brake master cylinder (4) mounted on the frame with the pipe (5). The master cylinder's piston (3) is operated by the driver by pressing the brake pedal (1) to push the push rod (2), and the brake shoes are opened by the operating hydraulic wheel cylinder to generate a braking torque.

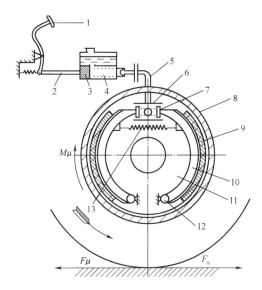

Fig. 3-5 Drum brake system

Disc Brake

In a disc brake with calipers, the fixed friction elements are one or more pairs of calipers with small friction linings on either side of the disc. Caliper disc brake is widely used in cars and light duty vehicles. Its advantages are good heat dissipation, low thermal decay and good thermal stability. It is most suitable for front-wheel brakes of cars with high requirements for braking performance. This is because the braking force of the front wheels is required to be larger and the rear wheels are often equipped with drum brakes.

Part Ⅱ Skill Training

Circuit Identification

Read the circuit diagram of AUDI A4(2009)'s brake light switch and answer the following two questions(Fig. 3-6).

(1)What are the main functions of each ECU?

(2)Within the brake light switch why need two different switches(one normally open switch, one normally closed switch)?

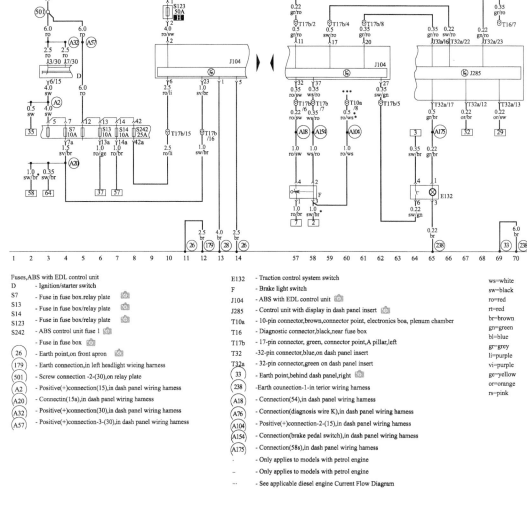

Fig. 3-6 Circuit diagram of AUDI A4(2009)'s brake light switch

Part III Exercises

Text Review

Exercise 1: Translate the following phrases into Chinese or English.

1. 从动盘 _____
2. _____ Pressure plate
3. 膜片弹簧 _____
4. _____ Releasing bearing
5. 主缸 _____
6. _____ Pedal adjust bolt
7. 工作缸 _____
8. _____ Push rod
9. 单向离合器 _____
10. _____ Brake drum

Exercise 2: Mark the following statements with T (True) or F (False) according to the passage.

(   ) 1. The frame is a structure similar to a bridge between various axles, and it is the installation basis of the whole automobile.

(   ) 2. The torque converter of the automatic transmission is installed between the flywheel and the planetary transmission mechanism.

(   ) 3. For an FF vehicle (front engine, front-wheel-drive) equipped with an manual transmission, the power delivery flow is: Engine → Clutch → Manual Transmission → Propeller shaft → Differential → Vehicle axle → Wheel.

(   ) 4. The function that the automobile suspension could realize is change the power of the engine.

(   ) 5. If the booster of the vehicle with power steering system fails, the vehicle cannot be turned.

Exercise 3: Translate the following paragraph into Chinese.

The vehicle chassis consists of a driveline, a running system, a steering system and a braking system. The driveline is used to transmit the power from the engine to the driving wheels, so that the road surface generates a traction force on the driving wheels to propel the vehicle. The running system is used to integrate various assemblies and components of the vehicle into one body to support the entire vehicle and ensure driving.

Part Ⅳ Listening and Speaking

After-Sales Call Back

Dialogue 1

A: Hello Mr. King, this is Michael from Johnson's Garage. Have I caught you in the middle of anything?

B: Ah, good morning. Anything I can do for you?

A: The purpose of my call is that we would like to know how do you like your new Honda Pilot.

B: Everything goes quite well.

A: That's nice. And I just have a couple of questions if you have a couple of minutes to talk.

B: Go ahead.

A: Thanks a lot. Are you satisfied with the quality of the Pilot you bought?

B: Yes. It is good.

A: Thank you. And are you satisfied with the overall performance of our sales representatives?

B: Yes. They are nice and helpful.

A: It is so kind of you to say so. Is there anything else we can do for you to help you know better of your car?

B: No, none for the moment, thank you!

A: Then do you have any suggestions about how we can improve our services?

B: No. Staff in the garage is very easy to work with and professional.

A: So glad to hear that. Thank you so much for your kind replies. Have a good day, Mr. King. You may call us or come to our garage anytime you have any questions about the car.

B: I will. Bye.

Dialogue 2

A: Thanks for calling Johnson's Garage. This is Michael. How may I help you?

B: This is Karry King. I bought a Honda Pilot from your garage last month.

A: Ah, yes. Good morning, Mr. King. How are you going on with the Pilot?

B: It runs smoothly overall, but it makes some noise when it makes turns. Maybe I should have it checked up at the garage.

A: It is a good idea. When will it be convenient for you to come by? We can make an appointment.

B: I will be free this Friday afternoon.

A: OK. Let me check the schedule. The working floor is available at 2 and 4 this Friday afternoon. Which time will be right for you?

B: 2 p.m. I think.

A: All right. It is done. You may come for the noise problem at 2 p.m. this Friday. And you should be at our garage between 1:45 and 2:15, or the working floor may be occupied by some car else. Please bring with you your driver's license and maintenance manual. I will call you Friday morning just to make sure that time is still good for you.

B: All right. Thank you!

A: Thanks again and I look forward to seeing you Friday at 2 p.m.!

Module 4 Electronic Control System

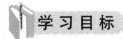

(1) 能够用英语介绍电控燃油喷射系统的部件;
(2) 能够用英语描述电控燃油喷射系统的作用和工作原理;
(3) 能够用英语介绍电子点火系统的部件;
(4) 能够用英语描述电子点火系统的作用和工作原理;
(5) 能够用英语介绍防抱死制动系统的部件;
(6) 能够用英语描述防抱死制动系统的作用和工作原理;
(7) 能够用英语介绍电动助力转向的部件;
(8) 能够用英语描述电动助力转向的作用和工作原理。

10 课时。

Part Ⅰ Reading Materials

Passage1 Electronic Control Fuel Injection

Electronic controlled fuel systems of gasoline engines consist mainly of the gasoline tank, fuel pump, fuel filter, fuel pipes (inlet pipes and return pipes), fuel injectors and fuel pressure regulator. See Fig. 4-1.

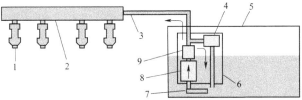

Fig. 4-1 Fuel supply system

1-Fuel injector /fjuəlin'dʒektə/   喷油器
2-Fuel distribution /'dɪstrɪ'bju:ʃn/ pipe   燃油分配管

3-Fuel input /ˈɪnpʊt/ pipe　　　　　　　　　进油管
4-Fuel pressure regulator /ˈregjuleɪtə(r)/　　油压调节器
5-Fuel tank /tæŋk/　　　　　　　　　　　　油箱
6-Fuel pump and filter cleaner assembly/əˈsembli/　燃油泵和滤清总成
7-Fuel inlet /ˈɪnlet/ filter　　　　　　　　　燃油进油滤网
8-Electrical /ɪˈlektrɪkl/ fuel pump　　　　　电动燃油泵
9-Fuel filter　　　　　　　　　　　　　　燃油滤清

Fuel is drawn from the fuel tank and pressurized to approximately 350kPa by the electric fuel pump. Passing through the fuel filter to remove impurities, the pressurized fuel flows to the fuel distribution pipe located above the engine. The fuel distribution pipe is connected to the fuel injectors installed in the intake manifold. The fuel injector is a kind of solenoid valve, controlled by the engine control unit (ECU). When energized, the fuel injector opens. The pressurized fuel is atomized and sprayed into the intake manifold to mix with air inside. During the intake stroke, the mixture is introduced into the cylinder.

Electric Fuel Pump

The plate impeller type electric fuel pump is a common electric fuel pump. At one end of the impeller type electric fuel pump casing is the fuel inlet, and the fuel outlet is on the other end.

The rotor (impeller) on the same side as the oil inlet is rotated at high speeds by the direct current motor located in the middle of the pump casing. When the pump is working, the fuel in the grooves rotates at a high speed along with the rotor. The fuel pressure at the fuel outlet is increased due to the effect of the centrifugal force. At the same time, certain vacuum is generated at the inlet to make the fuel flow through the filter screen at the inlet and to be absorbed into the fuel pump, which is pumped out from the space around the motor through the outlet after compression.

Fuel Filter

The purpose of a fuel filter is to remove dirt from the fuel, as the dirt can clog the fuel injectors. The fuel filter is installed in the fuel delivery pipe downstream to the electric fuel pump, generally with a service life of more than 40,000km.

Fuel Distribution Pipe

The distributor fuel pipe is adopted to deliver fuel to fuel injectors of various cylinders in a uniform and pressure-equalizing way. It plays roles such as fuel and pressure storage, avoidance of fuel pressure fluctuation and ensurance of providing equalizing fuels to various fuel injectors.

Fuel Injector

Fuel injectors are installed in the intake manifold and controlled by the ECU, with their nozzles facing the intake valves. Inside the fuel injector, there is a solenoid which is connected via a harness to the ECU. When the solenoid is energized by ECU, the resulting magnetic force picks up the armature and the needle valve. Thus the nozzle is open. Fuel under pressure is rapidly driven out of the nozzle, via the circular clearance between the needle-shaped plunger and the nozzle. And the fuel is atomized then mixes with air. During the intake stroke, the air-fuel mixture is introduced into the cylinder.

Fuel Pressure Regulator

The fuel pressure regulator is generally installed on one end of the distributor fuel pipe, and a fuel inlet of which is connected to the distributor fuel pipe, and the fuel outlet on the bottom is connected to the fuel return pipe. The upper vacuum interface is connected to the intake manifold through a flexible pipe.

The fuel pressure regulator is adopted to adjust the fuel pressure in the fuel pipe, so as to ensure that ECU can control the fuel injection quantity accurately by controlling the length of the fuel injection time.

Passage 2 Electronic Control Ignition

The electronically controlled ignition system is mainly composed of battery, ignition controllers, ignition coils, and spark plugs and etc. See Fig. 4-2.

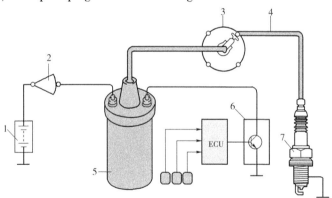

Fig. 4-2 Ignition system

1-Battery /ˈbætri/　　　　　　　　　蓄电池
2-Ignition switch /ɪgˈnɪʃən switʃ/　　　点火开关
3-Distributor /dɪˈstrɪbjətə(r)/　　　　分电器
4-High voltage /ˈvəʊltɪdʒ/ cable　　　高压线
5-Ignition coil /ɪgˈnɪʃən kɔɪl/　　　　点火线圈
6-ignitor /ɪgˈnaɪtə/　　　　　　　　　点火器
7-Spark /spɑːk/ plug　　　　　　　　火花塞

The electronically controlled ignition system accurately obtains various operating parameters of the engine through various sensors, and precisely controls the ignition advance angle through electronic control, so that the ignition advance angle of the engine under various operating conditions and usage conditions can be closer to the corresponding optimal ignition advance angle.

Battery

The battery and the generator (the battery works at start-up and the generator works after start-up) provide the required power to the ignition system.

Ignition Coil

The role of ignition coil is to convert the low voltage of the power supply of 12V to the high voltage of 15-30kV required for ignition.

An ignition coil can be classified to 2 types, namely open magnetic circuit ignition coil and closed magnetic circuit ignition coil, as per the type of magnetic circuit applied.

Spark Plugs

The role of spark plugs is to introduce high-voltage electricity into the combustion chamber of the cylinder to produce spark ignition mixture.

The spark plug is composed of a wiring nut (connected to a high voltage cable), an insulator, a center electrode, a sealing gasket, a shell, a side electrode, etc.

Ignition controller

Ignition controller includes breakers, distributors, capacitors, and the spark advance mechanism. Breakers are used to turn on/off the primary circuit of the ignition coil; the distributor includes the distributor cap and the distributor head.

They are used to send the high voltage generated by the ignition coil to the spark plug of each cylinder according to their working order of the engine.

Passage 3 Anti-lock Braking System

ABS is a set of control system added on the basis of the traditional braking system to prevent the wheel from being locked when braking. It mainly consists of wheel speed sensor, ABS actuator, ABS electric control unit and ABS warning light. See Fig. 4-3.

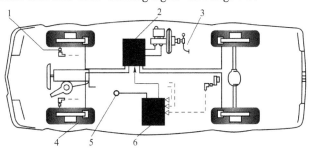

Fig. 4-3 Braking system

1-Wheel speed sensor /hwiːl spiːd'sensə/ 　　　轮速传感器
2-Hydraulic regulator /haɪ'drɔːlɪk'regjuleɪtə/ 　液压调节器
3-Brake pedal /breik'pedl/ 　　　　　　　　　制动踏板
4-Brake 　　　　　　　　　　　　　　　　　制动器
5-ABS warning light 　　　　　　　　　　　　ABS 故障警告灯
6-ABS electronic/ɪ'lektrɒnɪk/ control units 　　　ABS 电控单元

The brake light switch is installed next to the brake pedal. When the driver steps on the brake pedal, the brake light switch is turned on, the brake signal is input to the ABS ECU, and the brake light circuit at the rear of the sedan is connected.

Each wheel is equipped with a wheel speed sensor, which inputs the speed signals of each wheel to the electronic control unit (ECU) in time. ECU is the control center of the ABS. It monitors and judges the motion state of each wheel according to the signals inputted by each wheel speed sensor, and forms a response control command, and then issues a control command to the brake pressure regulator in due time; the brake pressure regulator is an actuator in ABS, which is an independent device composed of a pressure regulating solenoid valve assembly, an electric oil pump assembly and a liquid accumulator, etc. It is connected to the brake master cylinder (master pump, the same below) and each brake wheel cylinder (sub-pump, the same below) through the brake line. The brake pressure regulator is controlled by the electronic control unit and adjusts the brake pressure of each brake wheel cylinder. Under different road attachment conditions, 4-10 regulating cycles per second are carried out to ensure that the wheels do not lock during braking and that the wheel slip rate is within a reasonable range. The warning device includes a brake warning light and an ABS warning light on the dashboard.

Wheel Speed Sensor

Function of wheel speed sensor: detect wheel speed and input speed signal into ECU, suitable for slip rate control method. At present, the wheel speed sensors used in ABS system mainly include electromagnetic type and hall type.

ABS Actuator: Brake Pressure Regulator

The brake pressure regulator automatically adjusts the brake pressure of the wheel brakes via solenoid valves according to the ABS electronic control unit instructions. According to different brake systems, brake pressure regulators can be divided into hydraulic brake pressure regulators and pneumatic brake pressure regulators.

ABS Electronic Control Unit

Electronic control unit (ECU) is the control center of ABS. Its main function is to receive the sensor signal and process it, judge whether the wheel is locked, and then issue a brake pressure adjustment control command to the brake pressure regulator.

ECU generally consists of four basic circuits: sensor input amplifier circuit, operation correction circuit, output control circuit and safety protection circuit.

Passage 4 Electric Power Steering System

As shown in Fig. 4-4, electric power steering (EPS) uses a DC motor as a power source, and the ECU controls the magnitude and direction of the motor torque based on signals provided by sensors such as a torque sensor and a vehicle speed sensor. The torque of the motor is increased by the reducer (decreasing the speed) under the action of the electromagnetic clutch, and then applied to the steering mechanism of the car to obtain a steering force that is compatible with the working conditions.

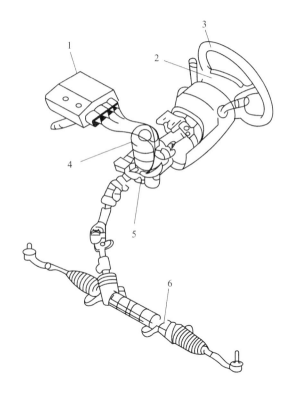

Fig. 4-4 Steering system

1-EPS ECU 电动助力转向系统控制单元
2-Steering wheel angle sensor /ˈæŋglˈsensə/ 转向角度传感器
3-Steering wheel 转向盘
4-Steering DC motor /ˈməʊtə(r)/ 转向直流电机
5-Steering torque /tɔːk/ sensor 转向力矩传感器
6-Steering gearbox /ˈɡɪəbɒks/ 转向器

The principle of control is that when the vehicle speed is low, the required steering force should be small and when the vehicle speed is high, the steering force required for steering should be appropriately increased.

Steering Gearbox

Its function is to increase the force transmitted from the steering wheel to the knuckle and change the direction of force transmission.

It is used to turn the rotary movement of steering wheel to the swing of steering rocker arm or straight reciprocating motion of rack shaft to control the swing of steering wheel

EPS ECU

EPS ECU is the core component of electronic power steering system, which is mainly used to receive various data of sensors and control the work of steering power motor according to each data to achieve the effect of steering power.

Steering Wheel Angle Sensor

Steering wheel angle sensor, a component of EPS, is mainly installed in the steering wheel under the direction of the column. It mainly measures the steering wheel's "rotation angle" when the car turns.

Steering Torque Sensor

The steering power moment is calculated by calculating the torque applied by the driver to the steering torque sensor, so as to achieve the effect of steering power.

Steering DC Motor

EPS system can be divided into steering shaft booster, gear booster and rack booster according to the installation position of power motor. Steering shaft power-assisted EPS motor is fixed on one side of the steering shaft and connected with the steering shaft through deceleration mechanism to directly drive the steering shaft power-assisted steering. Gear-assisted EPS motor and deceleration mechanism are connected with pinion to directly drive the gear-assisted steering. Rack EPS motor and deceleration mechanism directly drive rack to provide power.

Part Ⅱ Skill Training

Circuit Identification

Read the circuit diagram of Toyota Corolla's EPS and answer the following two questions (Fig. 4-5).

(1) Which sensor signals are received by EPS ECU?

(2) How does speed signal affect EPS actuator?

Module 4 Electronic Control System

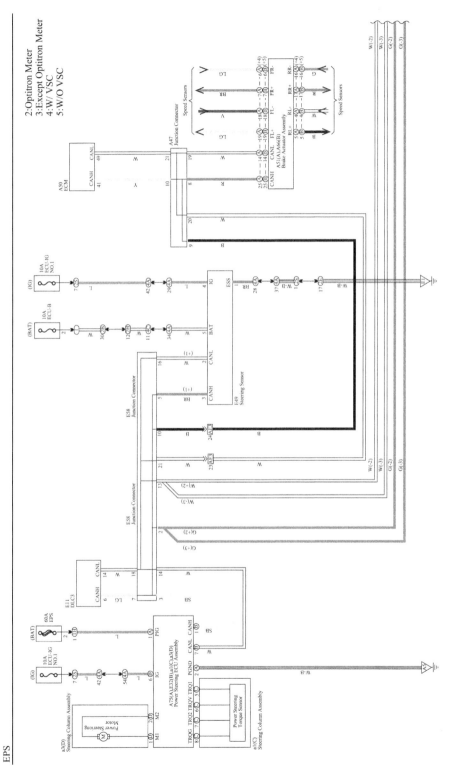

Fig. 4-5 Circuit diagram of Toyota Corolla's EPS

Part Ⅲ Exercises

Text Review

Exercise 1: Translate the following phrases into Chinese or English.

1. _____   Fuel injector
2. 燃油分配管   _____
3. _____   Fuel input pipe
4. 油压调节器   _____
5. _____   Fuel tank
6. 分电器   _____
7. _____   Fuel inlet filter
8. 制动踏板   _____
9. _____   Fuel filter
10. 转向盘   _____

Exercise 2: Mark the following statements with T(True) or F (False) according to the passage.

(   )1. The electronic control system of engines can be divided into the electronic fuel injection system, ignition control system, intake control system, emission control system and fault diagnosis system.

(   )2. Main purpose of the electronic fuel injection system (EFI system) is to control the fuel injection amount of injector, hence the concentration of air-fuel fixture.

(   )3. Using the engine operation data measured by various sensors, such as vehicle speed, throttle opening, coolant temperature and intake flow. ECU calculates out the ignition advance angle that best suits the current operating mode of the engine.

(   )4. If the Steering DC motor is damaged, the rack and pinion device cannot function.

(   )5. When the driver steps on the brake pedal, the brake light switch is turned on, the brake signal is input to the ABS ECU, and the brake light circuit at the rear of the sedan is connected.

Exercise 3: Translate the following paragraph into Chinese.

Electronic control system of gasoline engine is a generic term for all electronic control devices that are installed in or connected to the engine. Purpose of the electronic control system is to control the operation of various systems of the engine so that the engine exhibits high power performance and fuel economy with low pollutant emission.

Part Ⅳ Listening and Speaking

Daily Maintenance

Dialogue 1

A: Hi. I need some help. I′m confused with some minor problems.

B: Hi. Good afternoon, Madam. It is my pleasure.

A: How often should I change the oil in my car?

B: Normally you should change your oil every 5,000km or once half a year.

A: Should I rotate the tires?

B: Yes, it is strongly recommended. Rotating your tires will keep them in good condition and keep you safe.

A: What type of gas should I put into it?

B: I need to check your car manual. You don't want to put the wrong gas in your car, do you? It might ruin it.

A: OK. Then should I get tune ups?

B: Tune ups are good and you may find something that needs to be replaced but you would normally not know about.

A: The last question. Should I keep it outside or in my garage?

B: Better to keep it in your garage if you have one. It will keep your car safe from the bad weather. But if you don't have one, you may just keep it in your driveway.

A: Got it. Thank you so much!

B: You are welcome. This is our business card. Come by or call in whenever you need.

Dialogue 2

A: hello, Mr. Wang. This is Micheal speaking from Johnson's Garage. Can you spare me some minutes?

B: Sure. Go ahead.

A: Our records remind me that your Honda Pilot bought from our garage has been in use for 2 years with a mileage of about 30,000 miles. So we suggest that you take it to our garage and tune it up.

B: Yeah. A good idea, but how long will it take and what will be done?

A: General upkeep includes changing oil and the oil filter, aligning the wheels and cleaning valves, which will take about 2 hours. When will you find time to come by?

B: I will be free this Friday morning. I will come then.

A: Er, I am sorry but we are fully engaged then. Can we make it Friday afternoon or Saturday?

B: Saturday afternoon at 3:30 p.m..

A: Got it. I will reserve 3:30 p.m. Saturday for you. We will get ready and be expecting you then.

B: Thanks a lot.

A: One more tip. Remember to bring your driver's license and registration as well as the maintenance manual with you when coming. And I will call to remind you on Saturday morning.

B: All right. Thank you!

A: Have a nice day. Bye.

Module 5　Automotive Electrical Equipment

(1) 能够用英语介绍起动系统的部件;
(2) 能够用英语描述起动系统的作用和工作原理;
(3) 能够用英语介绍电动刮水器的部件;
(4) 能够用英语描述电动刮水器的工作原理;
(5) 能够用英语介绍前照灯系统的部件;
(6) 能够用英语描述前照灯的工作原理;
(7) 能够用英语介绍转向灯的部件;
(8) 能够用英语描述转向灯的工作原理。

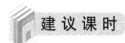

10 课时。

Part Ⅰ　Reading Materials

Passage 1　Starting System

　　To transit the engine from stationary state to working status, it is a must to rotate crankshaft of the engine with external force to inhale (or form) inflammable mixture and inflame and expand within the air cylinder, in this way, working cycles can be carried out automatically. The whole process from the crankshaft's starting to rotate under the external force to the engine's starting to conduct idle running automatically is called as starting of engine, and it is also the function of the starting system.

　　To start the engine, the engine should satisfy certain requirements. In addition to the requirements on compression of air cylinder, mixture concentration, strength of electric spark (gasoline engine) or ignition temperature (diesel engine), the starting system is required to provide starting torque and starting speed for the engine.

Module 5 Automotive Electrical Equipment

As shown in Fig. 5-1, at the time of starting, the ignition switch is rotated to ST position, the coil of starting relay is connected to close contact of starting relay, electromagnetic switch of starter is connected through 50 terminal, and connects 30 terminal and C terminal, namely, it connects cable of battery and motor in the starter to make the motor in the starter rotate and drive the engine to rotate and start.

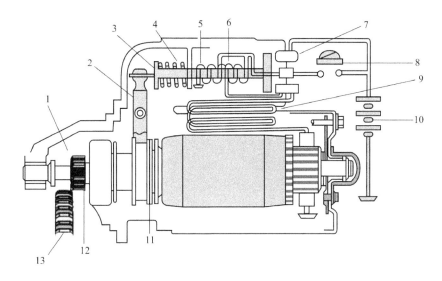

Fig. 5-1 Starting system

1-Drive gear /draivgiə/　　　　　　　　驱动齿轮
2-Shifting fork /'ʃiftiŋ fɔːk/　　　　　　拨叉
3-Movable core　　　　　　　　　　　活动铁芯
4-Offsetting spring /'ɔːfˌsetiŋ spriŋ/　　复位弹簧
5-Holding coil /'həʊldiŋkɔil/　　　　　　保持线圈
6-Sucking coil /'sʌkiŋkɔil/　　　　　　　吸引线圈
7-Terminal /'tɜːminl/　　　　　　　　　端子
8-Ignition switch /ɪg'nɪʃən switʃ/　　　点火开关
9-Field coil /fiːld kɔil/　　　　　　　　励磁线圈
10-Battery　　　　　　　　　　　　　　蓄电池
11-Screw thread spline /splain/　　　　螺纹花键
12-Clutch /klʌtʃ/　　　　　　　　　　　离合器
13-Flywheel ring gear /'flaiwiːl riŋ giə/　飞轮齿圈

Battery

The battery supplies the large current required by the starter.

Starting System

Electric starting system is composed of starter and control circuit (Fig. 5-1). Mainly including: battery, starter, starting relay and ignition switch (also known as starting switch for diesel engine). As for specific vehicle, it may consist of starting safety switch (or starting safety relay), starting block system relay and so on as well.

The function of the starter is to convert the electric power provided by battery to starting torque, drive flywheel of the engine to rotate through pinion gear and then make the engine start. The starter is composed of DC motor, transmission mechanism and control device. DC motor is composed of armature (rotor), magnetic pole (stator), commutator and electric brush and other main parts.

Armature

The rotating part of DC motor is called as armature, also known as rotor. The rotor is composed of iron core with excircle grooved laminated by silicon steel sheets, armature winding coils, armature shaft and commutator.

Stator

The magnetic pole is also known as stator in the starter, and consists of stator iron core and stator winding coil fixed in machine enclosure. The stator iron core is made of low-carbon steel and fixed on the machine enclosure of the starter with nut. The stator iron core is wound with stator winding coils (also known as excitation winding), and magnetic pole is generated after power connection. The stator iron core of DC permanent magnet motor is made of permanent magnet, without stator winding coils.

Electric Brush and Electric Brush Bracket

The electric brush bracket is frame construction in general. Thereinto, positive electric brush bracket is fixed on the end cover with insulation, and negative electric brush bracket is directly connected with end cover and grounded. The electric brush is placed in the electric brush bracket, and it is suppressed and formed by copper powder and graphite powder, being brownish black. The disk spring with strong elasticity on the electric brush bracket presses the electric brush to the commutator.

Passage 2　Windshield Wiper

The function of the windshield wiper is to remove rain, snow or dust from the windshield to ensure good visibility for the driver.

Windshield wipers contain two front windshield wiper and a rear windshield wiper. The electric wiper is mainly composed of a DC motor, a worm and gear reducer, a crank rocker mechanism (a crank, a link, a swinging rod, and a frame), a wiper arm, a wiper blade holder and a wiper blade. See Fig. 5-2.

Module 5 Automotive Electrical Equipment

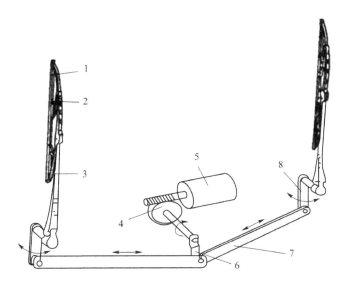

Fig. 5-2 Windshield wiper

1-Wiper blade /ˈwaipə bleid/   刮水片
2-Wiper blade holder /ˈhəʊldə(r)/   刮水片架
3-Wiper arm   刮水臂
4-Worm gear reducer /rɪˈdjuːsə/   蜗轮蜗杆减速器
5-Motor   电动机
6-Crank /kræŋk/   曲柄
7-Connecting rod /kəˈnektiŋ rɔd/   连杆
8-Rocker /ˈrɒkə(r)/   摇杆

Generally, the motor and the worm box are integrated to form the wiper motor assembly. The crank and the crank rocker mechanism converts the rotation of the worm into the oscillating motion of the swing arm, so that the wiper blade on the swing arm can wipe.

Wiper Motor

There are winding type wiper motor and permanent magnet type wiper motor. A permanent-magnet wiper motor is small in size, light in weight, simple in structure and is widely used.

A permanent-magnet wiper motor is mainly composed of the housing, permanent magnet, armature, brush mounting plate, reset switch (copper ring and contact), worm gear and worm.

The motor armature starts to rotate when it is powered. The worm gear drives the reducer. The worm drives the crank to rotate. The crank drives the wiper blade to oscillate from side to side through the link.

Fault Diagnosis of Slow Wiper Speed

If the wiper speed at any position is slower than normal, check if the wiper motor power line voltage is normal. If the voltage is low, check the connection terminals on the middle relay, the fuse and the control switch in the wiper circuit for firm connection and check the components for proper operation. If the voltage is normal, check whether the contact between the brush and the commutator on the wiper motor is in good condition, and whether the motor bearing and the worm are lubricated properly.

Passage 3 Light System

To guarantee the safety of car running, improve the car utilization, and reduce the traffic accidents and mechanical accidents, cars are all installed with many lighting devices and light signal systems, which are commonly known as light system.

Auto lighting system is mainly used for lighting the road, marking the car's width, interior lighting, meter checking and night repairing of a car running in night. The lighting system is composed of power source, lighting device and control part. Control part includes various light switches and relays, etc. Lighting device includes exterior lighting, interior lighting, and working lighting.

Exterior Lighting

Exterior lighting includes: headlight, front signal lamp, front turn signal lamp, and front fog lamp, etc. The existing cars basically adopt combination type lighting. The rear lighting includes backup light, license plate lamp, rearsignal light, braking signal light, front turn signal lamp, and rear fog lamp, etc. See Fig. 5-3.

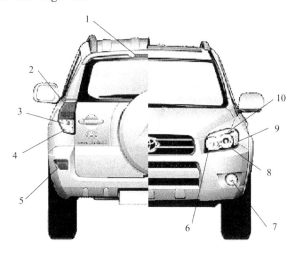

Fig. 5-3 Lights

1-High Mount /maʊnt/ Stop Lamp (LED)　　　高位制动灯（LED）
2-Stop light　　　制动灯
3-Taillight /ˈteɪllaɪt/　　　尾灯
4-Reversing /riˈvəːsiŋ/ light　　　倒车灯
5-Rear Fog Lamp　　　后雾灯
6-High beam /hai biːm/　　　远光灯
7-Front Fog lamp　　　前雾灯
8-Low beam　　　近光灯
9-Turn signal /ˈsignəl/　　　转向信号灯
10-Width lamp /widθ læmp/　　　示宽灯

Headlight

As the biggest light on the car, it is also known as headlamp, and it is installed on two sides of car head, used for lighting during the nighttime or on the road with dimly light.

Overtaking Lamp

There is no professional bulb in the overtaking lamp, and it is basically same to all cars that an overtaking lamp switch is set in the dimmer switch of headlight circuit. When dimmer switch is toggled to the highest position with hand, the overtaking lamp switch will be connected, and the high beam lamp will be on, the high beam lamp will become dark when the hand is relaxed.

Front Width Lamp

It is also known as clearance lamp, with white light. It is used for promoting the car position and width to other cars in the night. Also, it can light the road surface around the vehicle wheel.

Rear Width Lamp

It is also known as tail lamp, with red light. It is used for promoting the car position and width to other cars in the night. High-position width lamp and lateral width lamp are also available in some large passenger cars.

Front Fog Lamp

It is installed in the head of car and slightly lower than the headlight. The front fog lamp is used for improving the road lighting in the severe conditions like fog, snow, rainstorm or dust.

Rear Fog Lamp

It is a red signal lamp that is installed in the rear of car and has a higher light intensity than tail lamp. It functions to indicate the vehicle width and position for other road partici pants behind the car in fog, snow, rain or dusty weather and other environments with a lower visibility.

Turn Signal Lamp

Turn signal lamp is classified into front, rear turn signal lamp and left, right turn signal lamp. They are respectively installed on two ends of car as well as the front wing, with yellow light. When turn signal lamp is lightened, it indicates to the cars in the front and rear, as well as on the left and right that the car driver is turning or will change the lane direction.

Hazard Warning Lamp

There is no special hazard warning lamp on the car, and a hazard warning lamp switch is set in the vehicle lighting circuit. When the switch is connected, it can control all turn signal lamps to be on.

Brake Lamp

It is installed at the tail of vehicle, with red light. Many vehicles have their brake lamps and with lamps share the same bulbs. The brake lamp will be lit when the car brakes, to notify the vehicles behind of its braking, so as to avoid its collision with the vehicles behind.

License Plate Lamp

License plate lamp is above the license plate in the tail of car. It is used for lighting the license plate. When rear width lamp is on, the license plate lamp will also be on.

Reversing Lamp

It is installed in the tail of car, and it will be on when the ignition switch is connected, and gear shift lever is in the reverse gear position. It is used to provide additional lighting for the driver, so that the driver can see the rear part of car clearly while reversing in the night, which can also indicate the vehicles behind that the driver wants to back the car or is backing the car.

Instrument Lamp

It is used for lightening the instrument board in the night, so that the driver can see the instrument clearly and rapidly. When width lamp is on, instrument lamp will also be on.

Roof Light

It is used for lighting to the interior passengers, but it shall not cause the driver's dazzling. Generally, the interior lights of passenger cars are located in the middle of cab, so that the interior lighting is uniformly distributed.

Working Lamp

Working lamp includes: trunk lamp, hood lamp, and etc. The various indicator lamps and warning lamps on the instrument board are included.

Passage 4　Turn Signal Lamp

Turn signal lamp is mainly used for indicating the vehicle turning direction, to draw attentions of the traffic police, pedestrians and other drivers. In addition, flickering turn signal lamp is also used for the indication of danger warning. The turn signal lamp flickering is realized via flasher. Flasher is generally classified into heating wire type, capacitor type, transistor type and integrated circuit type based on the differences in structure and working principle.

As shown in Fig. 5-4, take the Toyota Corolla turn signal and hazard warning light circuit as an example. The circuit is mainly composed of battery, ignition switch, relay, turn signal flasher, turn signal lamp switch, danger warning lamp switch, anti-theft ECU and left/right turn signal lamps, etc.. When ignition switch is turned on, battery anode will provide power supply for internal electronic components of turn signal flasher via the contact of relay and terminal IG of turn signal flasher, and the current will return back to battery cathode via terminal GND.

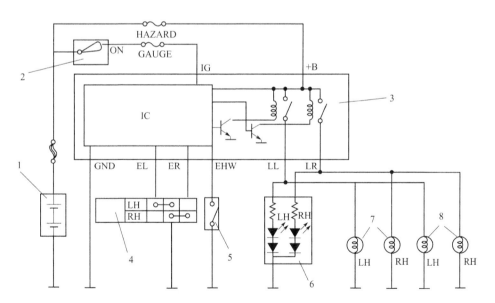

Fig. 5-4　Turn signal lamp

1-Battery　　　　　　　　　　　　　　蓄电池
2-Ignition switch /ɪgˈnɪʃən swɪtʃ/　　　点火开关

3-Flasher relay /ˈflæʃə ˈriːlei/   闪光继电器
4-Turn switch   转向灯开关
5-Hazard /ˈhæzəd/ warning switch   危险警报灯开关
6-Turn signal indicator /ˈɪndɪkeɪtə(r)/   转向信号指示灯
7-Front turn signal lamp   前转向信号灯
8-Rear turn signal lamp   后转向信号灯

At this time, if the turn signal lamp switch is toggled to the left turn position, a low voltage signal of bonding will be given to the turn signal flasher terminal EL. After turn signal flasher receives the signal, terminal IG and terminal LL will be connected via internal electronic components.

The current of left turn signal lamp and left turn signal indicator lamp is: battery anode → fusible wire → relay → turn signal flasher terminal IG → turn signal flasher terminal LL → front turn signal lamp LH, rear turn signal lamp LH, and left turn signal lamp and left turn signal lamp on the instrument boar, 4 lamps in total → bonding → battery cathode. Right turn signal lamp has basically the same working procedures.

Working principle of danger warning lamp is: whether ignition switch is connected or not, when danger warning lamp is closed, a low voltage signal of bonding is provided for turn signal flasher terminal EHW. After the turn signal flasher receives the signal, terminal + B will be respectively connected with the terminal LR and the terminal LL via the internal electronic components.

At this time, the current of danger warning lamp is: battery anode → fuse → turn signal lamp flasher terminal + B → terminal LL and terminal LR of turn signal lamp flasher → 8 lamps of front/rear, left/right, lateral turn signal lamp, and left/right turn signal lamp and signal lamp on instrument board → front turn signal lamp LH, rear turn signal lamp LH, and left turn signal lamp and left turn signal lamp on the instrument boar, 4 lamps in total → bonding → battery cathode. 6 turn signal lamps, including left/right, left/right and lateral turn signal lamps, flicker, and all turn signal lamps can flicker to play the role of danger warning lamp.

At the same time, left/right turn signal lamp and signal lamp on the instrument board will also flicker, to give the driver the information that the danger warning lamp is turned on.

Part II   Skill Training

Circuit Identification

Read the circuit diagram of Toyota Corolla's windshield wiper and answer the following two questions (Fig. 5-5).

Module 5 Automotive Electrical Equipment

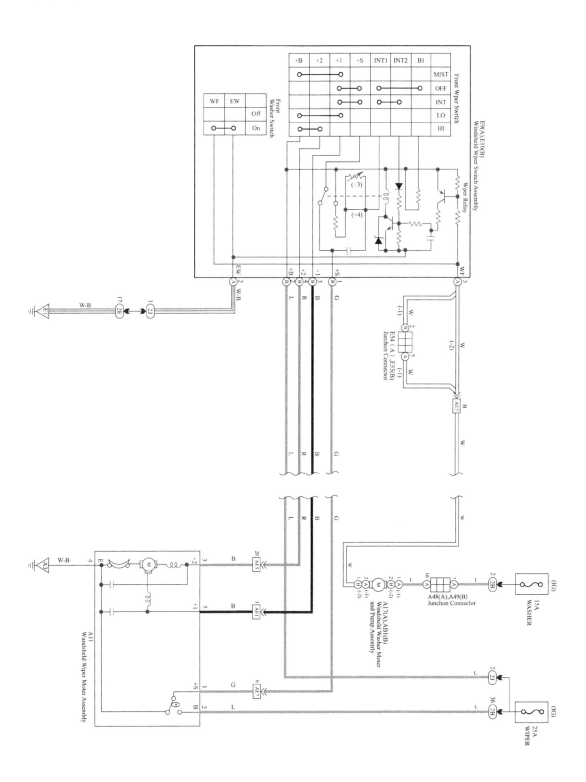

Fig. 5-5 Circuit diagram of Toyota Corolla's windshield wiper

(1) Analyze the working principle of wiper circuit.

(2) According to the circuit diagram, why after turning off the wiper switch, the wipers can return to their original positions?

Part Ⅲ   Exercises

Text Review

Exercise 1: Translate the following phrases into Chinese or English.

1. 刮水片 _____
2. _____ Battery
3. 刮水臂 _____
4. _____ Tail light
5. 电动机 _____
6. _____ Holding coil
7. 连杆 _____
8. _____ Rocker
9. 危险警报灯 _____
10. _____ Turn signal indicator

Exercise 2: Mark the following statements with T(True) or F(False) according to the passage.

(   )1. The starting system mainly includes the two parts, starter and control circuit.

(   )2. The drive device which enables the wiper to move is a crank rocker mechanism.

(   )3. Main signal equipment of auto signal system: turn signal lamp, rear lamp, brake lamp and reversing lamp, etc.

(   )4. Headlamp is composed of reflector, filament shield and bulb, three parts.

(   )5. When closing the directional lamp switch, a trigger signal will be provided, and integrated circuit will produce pulse signal and the triode is connected. Switch on relay coil.

Exercise 3: Translate the following paragraph into Chinese.

Starting system consists mainly of the starter, relay, switch, and protection equipment. Purpose of the starting system is to start the engine, from stationary to automatic rotation. Power-driven system includes power windows, power mirrors, power windscreen wipers, power seats, power sunroof, and centrally controlled door locks, which are all small equipments driven by motors.

Part Ⅳ Listening and Speaking

Service Advisor

Dialogue 1

A: Good afternoon! May I help you?

B: Good afternoon. I'm Kerry King. I take my car here for upkeep. Michael here has reserved 3 p.m. today for me.

A: Ah, yes, Mr. King. You are really punctual. It is great. Everything has been ready for the upkeep of your Honda Pilot.

B: Thank you!

A: Let us do a preliminary vehicle inspection.

B: All right.

A: May I get in and check up the interior devices and their functions?

B: Yes, please.

A: Thank you. The mileage is 29,765 miles, and the tank is half full. Lights, wipers and stereo all function well.

B: That is nice.

A: Now turn to the exterior. It is also in good condition, although it is inevitably covered with some dirt. We will offer a free car wash at the end of the upkeep.

B: It is really nice of you to do it.

A: You are welcome. Any problems come up when you drive it?

B: No.

A: Good. Later the technician will do a thorough examination and make sure the car is in sound condition. To keep the inner space from getting dirty, later we will cover the seats with seat covers. Do you leave any valuables inside the car? It is suggested that you carry them with yourself.

B: No, thanks. No valuables inside.

A: OK. Here is the pre-inspection checklist. Please confirm and sign here.

B: It is done.

A: Thank you. We will write the statement over the reception desk there. Please come this way.

Dialogue 2

A: Hi, Mr. King. Sorry to disturb you. I have a question for you.

B: Hum. What is it?

A: Did you ever clean the air-conditioner for your Pilot?

B: No, never. Anything wrong?

A: I suggest that you have it cleaned.

B: Why? There is nothing wrong.

A: Maybe not for the present. But 80% of the dust and bacteria will make their way through the filter into the air-conditioner when it is running. And passengers inside the car will be vulnerable to flu, tonsillitis, or even pneumonia when the dust or bacterial just pile up. So it is strongly suggested that the air-conditioner should be cleaned regularly.

B: Really? It sounds quite serious.

A: Indeed. Shall I register it for you? Our technician will clean it later.

B: OK! Just do what you recommend. And how often shall I clean the air-conditioner for my car?

A: Usually the filter should be cleaned once a month, and the whole gadget at least once a year. It needs to be cleaned when you know that the machine will be shut down for a long time or after a long time it has been shut down. Besides, it also needs to be cleaned when it is smelly in use.

B: All right. I got it. Thank you!

Module 6　Safety and Comfort System

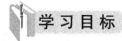

(1)能够用英语介绍辅助约束系统的部件;
(2)能够用英语描述辅助约束系统的作用和原理;
(3)能够用英语介绍汽车防盗系统的类型;
(4)能够用英语描述各类型防盗系统的工作原理;
(5)能够用英语介绍空调系统的部件;
(6)能够用英语描述空调系统各部件的作用和工作原理;
(7)能够用英语介绍多媒体播放及导航系统的部件;
(8)能够用英语描述多媒体播放及导航系统各部件的作用和工作原理。

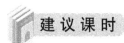

10 课时。

Part Ⅰ　Reading Materials

Passage 1　Supplemental Restraint System

Function of SRS

In order to protect passengers, Supplemental Restraint System opens instantly when the car collides, absorbs and mitigates the damage caused by the impact force.

Working Principle of SRS

The main components of SRS are shown in Fig.6-1. SRS can open the airbag instantly when the car collides, and provide protection for the driver and passengers in the same car with the safety belt, so it can effectively reduce the impact on the head and chest. In addition, the SRS side airbag system can protect the chest of passengers sitting in the driver's seat and the copilot's seat when side impact occurs, and the SRS curtain airbag system can protect the head of passengers sitting in the front and rear seats.

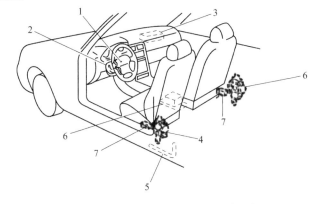

Fig.6-1　Supplemental restraint system(SRS)

1-Driver airbag modules /ˈmɒdʒʊlz/　　　　　　驾驶员安全气囊模块
2-Helical /ˈhelɪkl/ cable　　　　　　　　　　　螺旋电缆
3-Front passenger /ˈpæsɪndʒə(r)/ airbag module　前排乘客气囊模块
4-Seat belt tensioner-1 /ˈteʃənə/　　　　　　　安全带预张紧器-1
5-Seat belt tensioner-2　　　　　　　　　　　安全带预张紧器-2
6-Diagnostic /ˌdaɪəgˈnɒstɪk/ sensor unit　　　　诊断传感器单元
7-Side balloon /bəˈluːn/ sensor　　　　　　　　侧气囊传感器

Characteristics of SRS

(1) Only when the ignition switch is in ON or START position can the supplemental airbag work. When the ignition key is turned to ON position, the supplemental airbag warning lamp is lit. If the system works, the supplemental airbag warning light will be turned off in about 7 seconds.

(2) When side impact occurs, it can reduce the impact on head, face and neck. When the SRS curtain airbag is impacted by the side, the airbag installed on the side of the roof can be opened instantly to protect the passengers in front and rear seats effectively. The airbag not only alleviates the impact on the passenger's head and face caused by the collision, but also restrains the excessive bending of the neck and alleviates the injury to the neck.

(3) In the case of side impact, rear impact, rollover or low-severity frontal impact, the supplemental front airbag usually does not inflate. Always wear seat belts to reduce the risk or severity of injury in various accidents.

(4) The front passenger airbag will not be inflated when the front passenger airbag indicator lights up or the front passenger seat is empty. In addition, due to the danger of the airbag system and the need for proper use in order to make SRS system work, so for vehicles equipped with SRS airbag, in daily use, we need to pay attention to some matters. In order to ensure the safety of drivers and passengers, the seat belt should be fastened while ensuring the correct driving posture.

Passage 2 Car Security System

Function of Car Security System

Car Security System is a device installed on the car to increase the difficulty of car theft and prolong the time of car theft. As shown in Fig. 6-2, by matching the anti-theft device with the automobile circuit, it can prevent the vehicle from being stolen and violated, protect the car and realize various functions of the anti-theft device.

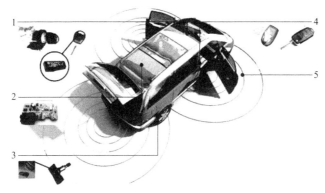

Fig. 6-2 Security system

1-(IMMO) Engine Immobilizer /ɪˈməʊbəlaɪzə/　　　发动机熄火防盗控制
2-(RF) Radio Frequency /ˈreɪdiəʊ ˈfriːkwənsi/　　　射频
3-(TPMS) Tire pressure monitoring /ˈmɒnɪtərɪŋ/ system　　　胎压检测系统
4-(RKE) Remote /rɪˈməʊt/ keyless entry　　　遥控开锁
5-(PKE) Passive /ˈpæsɪv/ Keyless Entry　　　无钥匙开锁和起动

The Type of Car Security System

With the progress of science and technology, in order to cope with the escalating means of car theft, people have developed various kinds of anti-theft devices with different structures. According to their structures, anti-theft devices can be divided into four categories: mechanical, chip, electronic and network.

Mechanical Type of Car Security System

The mechanical anti-theft is the simplest and cheapest type of Car Security System on the market, and its principle is very simple. It only locks the steering wheel and the control pedal or baffle handle. Its advantages are low price and easy installation, while its disadvantages are incomplete anti-theft, troublesome disassembly and assembly, and needing to be placed when not in use.

Chip Type of Car Security System

The basic principle of chip anti-theft is to lock the engine, circuit and oil circuit of the car, and can't start the car without the chip key. Digitized password weight rate is very low, and it is necessary to contact the car's password lock with the password key to unlock, thus eliminating the possibility of being scanned.

Chip-based anti-theft has developed to the fourth generation. It has special diagnostic function, that is, the authorized person can get the historical information of the anti-theft system when reading the secret key information. The number of authorized spare keys, time stamp and other background information in the system become part of the security of transceiver. Unique radio frequency identification technology can ensure that the system can correctly identify the driver under any circumstances, and can automatically identify the driver when the driver is approaching or away from the vehicle, and automatically open or close the car lock.

Electronic Type of Car Security System

Electronic anti-theft is a car anti-theft method that add electronic identification to the car lock, so that unlocking and matching keys need to input a password with more than a dozen numbers. It generally has remote control technology. It has the following four functions.

1. Anti-theft Alarm Function

This function means that the alarm will enter the alert state after the car owner locks the door remotely. If someone prizes the door or opens the door with a key, the alarm will be immediately triggered by the burglar alarm.

2. Safety Prompt Function for Unlocked Door

If the door is not locked properly after the automobile is extinguished, the lamp will flicker and the horn will honk until the door is closed.

3. Car Search Function

When a car owner seeks for a car with a remote controller, the horn sounds intermittently, accompanied by flashing lights.

4. Remote Control Central Door Lock

When the remote control transmits the correct signal, the central door lock opens or closes automatically.

GPS Type of Car Security System

The working principle of GPS is to use the receiving satellite transmitting signal and the ground monitoring equipment and the GPS signal receiving unit to form a global positioning system. The satellite constellation continuously transmits the three-dimensional position, velocity and time information of the dynamic target, to ensure that vehicles can receive signals from satellites at least at any place on the earth and at any time. GPS mainly relies on locking ignition or starting to achieve the purpose of anti-theft, but also through the GPS satellite positioning system, the location of the alarm place and the alarm vehicle can be silently transmitted to the alarm center.

Passage 3 Air Conditioning System

There are many kinds of refrigeration systems in the world. Among them, the expansion valve refrigeration system is most commonly used in cars. The main components of expansion valve refrigeration system are compressor, condenser, storage dryer, expansion valve and evaporator. See Fig. 6-3.

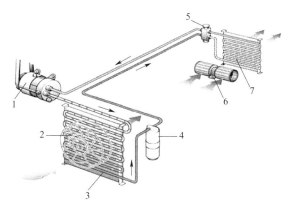

Fig. 6-3 Air conditioning system

1-Compressor /kəm'presə(r)/　　　　压缩机
2-Radiator /'reɪdi:ˌeɪtə/ fan　　　　散热器风扇
3-Radiator /'reɪdi:ˌeɪtə/　　　　　　散热器
4-Storage /'stɔ:rɪdʒ/ drying bottle　　储液干燥罐
5-H-shape expansion /ɪks'pænʃən/ valve　H 型膨胀阀
6-Air-blower /'eər bl'əʊər/　　　　　鼓风机
7-Evaporator /ɪ'væpəˌreɪtə/　　　　蒸发箱

Function of Air Conditioning System

(1) Adjust the temperature in the car;
(2) Adjusting the humidity in the vehicle;
(3) Adjust the air velocity in the car;
(4) Filtration and purification of air in vehicles.

Compressor

Compressor is the core component of refrigeration system. Its functions are to maintain refrigerant circulation in the refrigeration system by external force, inhale refrigerant vapor from evaporator at low temperature and low pressure, compress refrigerant vapor to increase its temperature and pressure, and send refrigerant vapor to condenser to realize heat exchange in the process of heat absorption and release.

Condenser

In order to better heat dissipation, the condenser is installed at the rear of the intake grille and in front of the engine radiator. The function of the condenser is to exchange the high temperature and high pressure gaseous refrigerant discharged by the compressor with the air outside the condenser, transform it into liquid refrigerant at high temperature and high pressure, and distribute the heat to the outside environment of the vehicle.

Drier Receiver

Drier receiver is used in expansion valve refrigeration system. Its main functions are: temporary storage of refrigerants, so that the refrigerant flow rate and refrigeration load are compatible; filter out the impurities in refrigerants, absorb the moisture in refrigerants, prevent dirty clogging and ice jam in refrigeration system pipelines, and protect equipment components from erosion.

Expansion Valve

Expansion valve is an important part of automotive air conditioning system, usually installed between dryer receiver and evaporator. Expansion valve makes liquid refrigerant of medium temperature and high pressure become gaseous mixture refrigerant through throttling, and then refrigerant absorbs heat in evaporator to achieve refrigeration effect. Expansion valve controls the flow rate of the valve through the change of the ground degree at the end of the evaporator to prevent the insufficient utilization of the evaporation area and cylinder knocking.

Evaporator

When the refrigeration system works, the high-pressure liquid refrigerant expands through the expansion valve and reduces the pressure. It turns into wet steam and enters the core tube of the evaporator to absorb the heat of the radiator and the surrounding air. The evaporator is usually installed in the bellows behind the dashboard, and the air outside the vehicle or inside the vehicle flows through the evaporator by the blower for cooling and dehumidification.

Work Principle of Refrigeration Systems

1. Compression Process

The compressor compresses the vapor refrigerant at low temperature and low pressure on the low side of the evaporator (temperature is about 0℃, pressure is about 0.15 MPa) into a vapor refrigerant at high temperature and high pressure (temperature is about 110℃, pressure is about 1.5 MPa), which is sent to the condenser for cooling.

2. Condensation Process

When the temperature is much higher than the external temperature, the high temperature and high pressure gaseous refrigerant sent to the condenser can heat out and exchange heat. The refrigerant is condensed into a liquid refrigerant with medium temperature and high pressure (temperature is about 60℃, pressure is 1.0-1.2MPa)

3. Expansion Process

The condensed liquid refrigerant enlarges the volume of refrigerant space through expansion valve, and its temperature and pressure drop sharply. It becomes a mixture of low temperature and low pressure gas and liquid refrigerant, so as to enter the evaporator and quickly absorb heat and evaporate. In the expansion process, flow control is carried out at the same time to supply refrigerant needed by the evaporator, so as to achieve the purpose of temperature control.

4. Evaporation Process

The mixture of gas and liquid refrigerants continuously absorbs heat and is vaporized by evaporator and transformed into low temperature and low pressure gas refrigerant (temperature is about 0℃, pressure is about 0.15MPa), which absorbs the heat of the air in the car.

Passage 4   Navigation System

The vehicle guidance system is composed of vehicle part, main control center, etc.. Its main components are shown in Fig.6-4.

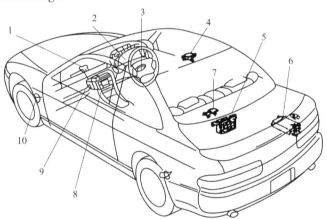

Fig.6-4   Navigation system

1-GPS-Antenna reception   GPS 天线接收
2-Vehicle speed sensor   车速传感器
3-Steering angle sensor   转向角度传感器
4-Geomagnetic sensor   地磁传感器
5-GPS-Receiver   GPS 接收器
6-CD-ROM Record player   CD-ROM 唱机
7-GPS-Receiving antenna   GPS 接收天线
8-LCD-Display   LCD 显示器
9-Navigation ECU   导航 ECU
10-Wheel speed sensor   车轮速度传感器

Main Control Center

The main control center is composed of radio, modem, computer system and electronic map. The radio of the main control center is used to receive the position information sent by the radio on the car, and at the same time, it can reverse control the car. The modem is responsible for the digital/analog conversion of anti-control commands and GPS information. After receiving the location information of the car, the computer system carries out simple preprocessing, and then packages the information according to the agreed communication protocol, and sends it to the workstation through RS 232. The workstation displays the location of the car on the vector electronic map data and has spatial query function.

Vehicle Part

The vehicle part is composed of GPS receiver, modem and radio. Some of them include self-regulated navigation device, speed sensor, gyroscope sensor, CD-ROM driver, LCD display and so on. GPS receivers are used to receive signals transmitted by GPS. The modem is used to control the data acquisition of GPS receiver, convert the data information into analog signal, and then send it to the main control center through the radio.

Working Principle of Automotive Electronic Navigation System

The GPS receiver receives the GFS satellite signal and finds out the coordinates, speed and time of the current point. When the car travels to the underground tunnel, the high-rise buildings, highways and other shelters and can't capture the GPS satellite signal, the system can automatically enter the autonomous navigation system.

Before driving, the driver inputs into the computer the names of the cities and streets to be visited using the keyboard. The computer will use the signals of the satellite system to guide. According to the measured data of the speed sensor and direction sensor, the position of the place to be visited is determined, and the best driving route of the place to be visited is indicated. During the driving process, the driver can use the display device in the car to observe at any time the map of the area where the car is located and the precise position of the car at any time on the map on the screen. The display constantly shows the distance to the destination.

Part Ⅱ Skill Training

Circuit Identification

Read the circuit diagram of CAMRY (EM02K0EC) air conditioner and answer the following two questions (Fig. 6-5).

(1) What are the main functions of ECU?

(2) What are the main sensors and actuators of the circuit diagram of CAMRY?

Module 6 Safety and Comfort System

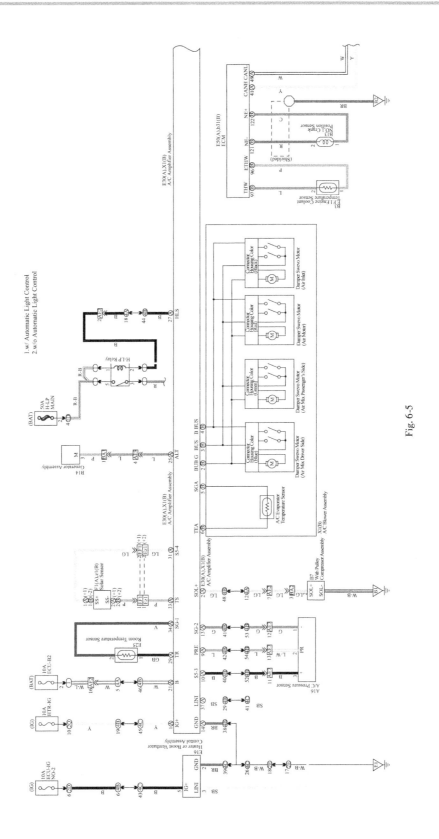

Fig. 6-5

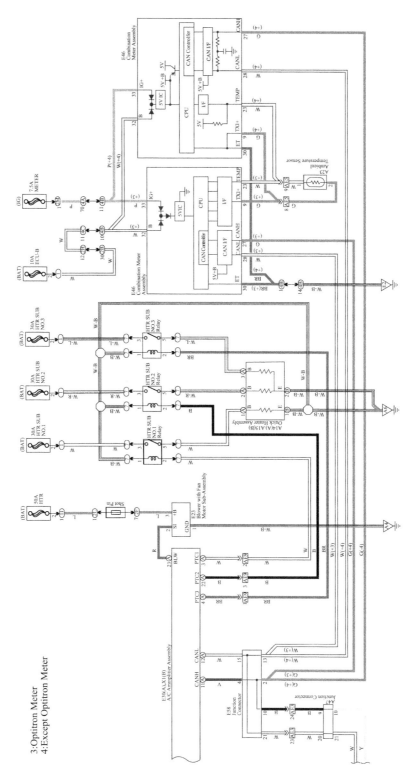

Fig. 6-5 Circuit diagram of CAMRY (EM02K0EC) air conditioner

Part III Exercises

Text Review

Exercise 1: Translate the following phrases into Chinese or English.

1. _____   Driver airbag modules
2. 安全带预张紧器   _____
3. _____   Side balloon sensor
4. 压缩机   _____
5. _____   Condenser
6. 膨胀阀   _____
7. _____   Evaporator
8. 遥控器   _____
9. _____   TV-Antenna
10. 速度传感器   _____

Exercise 2: Mark the following statements with T(True) or F(False) according to the passage.

(　　)1. In the whole process of refrigeration, constant displacement air conditioning compressor is always working.

(　　)2. When there is no refrigerant in the refrigeration system, the AC switch closed compressor will not work.

(　　)3. Expansion net can automatically control the opening and closing of electromagnetic clutch of compressor.

(　　)4. The installation position of the light sensor is generally on the cab dashboard and the bottom of the windshield glassy disease.

(　　)5. When the air conditioning refrigeration system works, the engine coolant temperature will be higher than usual.

Exercise 3: Translate the following paragraph into Chinese.

Automobile safety can be divided into active safety and passive safety. This module mainly introduces the Supplemental Restraint System (SRS) in passive safety. Supplemental Restraint System consists of airbags and seat belts. At the moment of a collision accident, the seat belt will tie the occupant tightly to the seat before moving forward, then lock the ribbon to prevent the occupant from leaning forward and effectively protect the safety of the occupant. The airbags can reduce the degree of injury caused by the second collision due to inertia.

Part Ⅳ　Listening and Speaking

Settlement and Delivery

Dialogue 1

A: Mr. King, sorry to keep you waiting. Here is the repair estimate for your Pilot.

B: Yes?

A: Please look here. Today we will change oil, oil filter and air filter, which costs $50, $5 and $10 respectively. In addition, there will be $8 for pulling a dent 5cm in depth and $64 for man-hour cost. All added, it is $137. Next time you can get 20% off for the man-hour fee and 10% off for the spare parts if you reserve in advance.

B: Is that all?

A: No. You mentioned there were odd sounds when pressing the brake pedal. There will be an extra charge after examination and maintenance.

B: OK.

A: Mr. King, it takes 2 hours or so to complete the upkeep, including half an hour of free car wash. And I will contact you right away when new problems come up. We will only take actions after your permission. Is that all right with you?

B: No problem.

A: Nice. So would you please sign here? This receipt is for you and it shall be produced when you pick up your car.

B: Got it.

A: Then will you wait here in our lounge or leave for a while?

B: I will leave and come back later for the car.

A: All right. I will call you when the car is ready.

B: See you!

Dialogue 2

A: Mr. King, may I have you receipt?

B: Here you are.

A: OK! Now let's go and check out your Pilot. We've cleaned up your Pilot in and out. And we replaced the brake pedal. There won't be odd sounds now. You may try it.

B: Hum, great!

A: You may check up the underhood now. It was also cleared. Oil, oil filter and air filter, all have been replaced. We have refilled the gas, lubricant, gear oil, hydraulic oil, brake fluid, coolant, glass cleaner as well as water. Anything else shall we do?

B: No. Thank you.

A: Nice. Mr. King, shall we put these worn parts into your trunk?

B: Yes. Please go ahead.

A: Now we can settle the bill over the reception desk. This way, please!

A: Here is the statement. It is $88, the same as we estimated. Please confirm and sign here.

B: All right. I will pay with Alipay.

A: No problem. Please show the QR code over the scanner. Here is the receipt. Thank you! Please remember to come for tune-up on a mileage of 35,000 km. Do reserve in advance, then you may enjoy the same service with less cost, and obtain better time arrangement as well.

B: I will. Thank you!

A: We will do a follow-up call next week. And you may come to any of our branches nationwide or call the numbers on this sheet whenever you need.

B: OK. It's very kind of you. I am leaving now.

A: Goodbye, Mr. King. Let me see you off.

Module 7　New Energy Vehicles

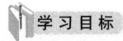

（1）能够用英语介绍纯电动汽车的类型；
（2）能够用英语描述纯电动汽车的组成；
（3）能够用英语介绍纯电动汽车的工作原理；
（4）能够用英语介绍混合动力汽车的类型及其特点；
（5）能够用英语介绍混合动力汽车的工作原理；
（6）能够看懂混合动力汽车电路图。

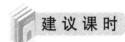

10 课时。

Part Ⅰ　Reading Materials

Passage 1　Types of Pure Electric Vehicles

Pure electric vehicle (BEV) is a vehicle powered entirely by rechargeable batteries (such as lead-acid batteries, nickel-cadmium batteries, nickel-hydrogen batteries or lithium-ion batteries). Its main composition is shown in Fig. 7-1.

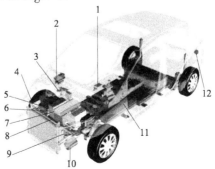

Fig. 7-1　Pure electric vehicle

1-Data collection terminal /ˈtɜːmɪnl/   数据采集终端
2-Complete vehicle controller   整车控制器
3-Fast filling /ˈfɪlɪŋ/   快充口
4-Low pressure fuse /fjuːz/ box   低压保险盒
5-Motor controller   电机控制器
6-High voltage /ˈvəʊltɪdʒ/ box   高压盒
7-DC/DC   直流/直流
8-Charger /ˈtʃɑːdʒə(r)/   充电机
9-Electric vacuum /ˈvækjuəm/ pump   电动真空泵
10-Vacuum tank   真空罐
11-Power battery /ˈbætri/ pack   动力电池包
12-Slow filling   慢充口

Pure electric vehicles come in a variety of different classification methods. According to the number of power system components and the layout, pure electric vehicles can be divided into the following types.

Conventional (Traditional) Electric Vehicle

The power transmission route is shown in the diagram [Fig. 7-2a)]. This kind of electric vehicle can be directly refitted from fuel-fired vehicle. Its characteristic is that the traditional internal combustion engine and fuel system are replaced by the electric bumper and battery system. Because the transmission, final drive and differential of traditional internal combustion engine are retained, the requirement for the motor is less and a smaller motor can be selected.

Variable Speed Electric Vehicle

The power transmission route is shown in the diagram [Fig. 7-2b)]. This kind of electric vehicle is characterized by replacing the traditional internal combustion engine and fuel system with the motor and battery system, and removing the transmission of the traditional internal combustion engine vehicle. The motor is directly connected to the transmission shaft, and the variable speed function is realized through the control of the motor. Although the weight and transmission loss of this type of electric vehicle are reduced, the size of the motor is larger.

Differential-Free Electric Vehicle

The power transmission route is shown in the diagram [Fig. 7-2c)]. The characteristic of this kind of electric vehicle is that the motor is directly connected to the left and right driving half axles. It has simple structure, reduces the weight and transmission loss of the whole vehicle, and achieves the distribution of the differential speed and driving force between the left and right wheels through the control of the motor.

Electric Wheeled Electric Vehicles

This kind of electric vehicle mainly consists of stator, permanent magnet, encoder, motor coil, bearing, planetary gear and brake hub, as shown in the diagram [Fig. 7-2d]. It is characterized by no power transmission device, which directly connects the driving motor to the driving wheel. It has the largest space utilization and no transmission loss. However, the control accuracy of the driving motor is required to be high, and the speed difference between the left and right wheels is required to meet the requirements of vehicle driving, especially when turning.

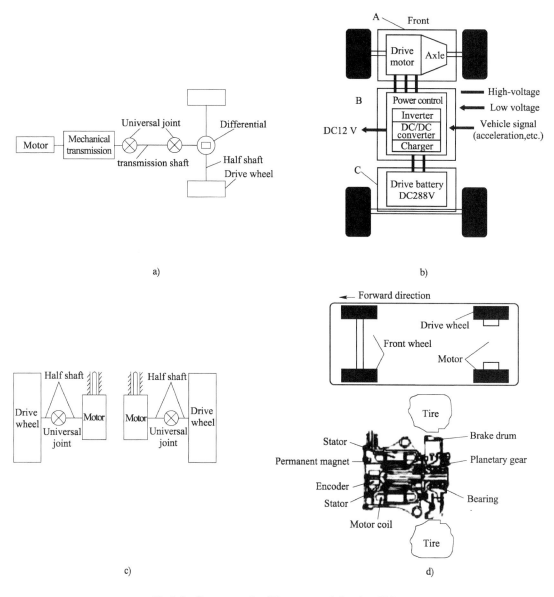

Fig. 7-2 Power routes for different types of electric vehicles

Module 7　New Energy Vehicles

Passage 2　The Structure and Working Principle

Structure

As shown in Fig. 7-3, pure electric vehicles are equipped with storage batteries, motors, motor control devices and energy management systems. The way of energy supplement is charging, which can be carried out in charging stations or parking lots. The chargers used in charging stations are mostly fast chargers. Because electric motors can generate electricity when they are dragged, pure electric vehicles generally have energy recovery (regeneration) systems that can recover deceleration and downhill energy.

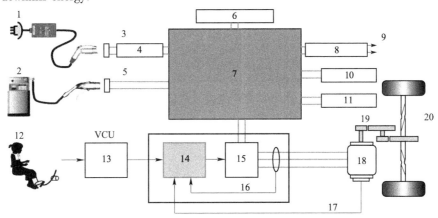

Fig. 7-3　Working principle

1-Slow charging /tʃɑːdʒɪŋ/　　　　　　慢速充电
2-Fast charging　　　　　　　　　　　快速充电
3-Slow charging plug /plʌg/　　　　　　慢速充电插头
4-Car charging　　　　　　　　　　　车载充电
5-Fast charging plug　　　　　　　　　快速充电插头
6-High voltage battery　　　　　　　　高电压电池
7-High voltage control box　　　　　　高压控制盒
8-DC/DC converter /kən'vɜːtə(r)/　　　DC/DC 转换器
9-14V output /'aʊtpʊt/　　　　　　　　14V 输出
10-Air conditioner /eə(r) kən'dɪʃənə/　　空调
11-Heater /'hiːtə(r)/　　　　　　　　　加热器
12-Driver　　　　　　　　　　　　　驾驶员
13-Vehicle controller　　　　　　　　　整车控制器
14-Motor controller　　　　　　　　　电机控制器
15-Power module /'paʊə 'mɔdjuːl/　　　功率模块
16-Current sensor /'kʌrənt 'sensə/　　　电流传感

17-Rotation /rəʊ'teɪʃn/ temperature signal　　旋变温度信号
18-Motor　　电机
19-Reduction /rɪ'dʌkʃn/ device　　减速器
20-Drive shaft　　驱动轴

Working Principle

As shown in Fig. 7-4, pure electric vehicle is powered by the energy of the battery that causes the motor to drive the vehicle forward. The working principle of electric vehicles: battery → current → power regulator → motor → power transmission system → driving the car. During the working process, the battery supplies current, which is regulated by the power regulator and then output to the motor, and then the torque is supplied by the motor, and the wheel is driven by the transmission device to drive the vehicle.

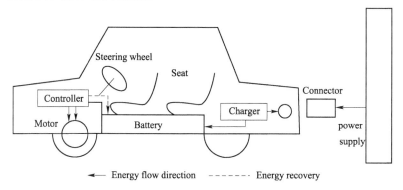

Fig. 7-4　Pure electric vehicle

Regenerative Braking

The regenerative braking of an electric vehicle is to use the electric brake of the electric motor to generate a reverse torque to slow down or stop the vehicle. For induction motors, electrical brakes have reverse brake, DC brake and regenerative brake. Among them, only regenerative braking can be achieved to recover energy during braking. The essence is that the rotating frequency of the rotor of the motor exceeds the power frequency of the motor, and the motor operates in a power generating state, converting mechanical energy into electrical energy to charge the battery through a reverse freewheeling diode of the inverter.

Passage 3　Types of Hybrid Electric Vehicles

Hybrid Electric Vehicle (HEV) is an electric vehicle equipped with both electric drive system and auxiliary power unit. The auxiliary power unit is a gasoline engine or diesel engine with mature technology. Its main composition is shown in Fig. 7-5. The main advantages of hybrid electric vehicle are that the engine works in the economic working area, with low emission and low fuel consumption. When the engine is not working at full load and acceleration, the noise is low. It can also recover braking energy and utilize existing fuel facilities. HEV is an important technical measure adopted by the contemporary automobile industry to protect the atmospheric environment and to utilize resource.

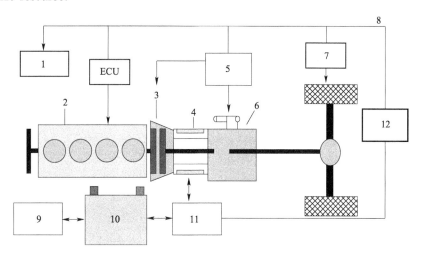

Fig. 7-5 Hybrid electric vehicle

1-Instrument /'ɪnstrəmənt/ 仪表
2-Engine /'endʒɪn/ 发动机
3-Automatic /ˌɔːtə'mætɪk/ clutch 自动离合器
4-ISG motor 集成起动/发电一体化电机
5-Clutch controller 离合控制器
6-AMT 机械式自动变速器
7-ABS 防抱死制动系统
8-Local /'ləʊkl/ CAN 局部 CAN
9-Vehicle controller 整车控制器
10-Energy storage /'stɔːrɪdʒ/ unit controller 储能单元控制器
11-Energy storage unit 储能单元
12-Motor Controller 电机控制器

According to the different configuration of the power system, it can be divided into series, parallel and hybrid type.

Series Hybrid Power System

The structure of series hybrid power system is shown in Fig. 7-6. Its working principle is that the engine drives the generator to generate electricity. Part of the electricity generated is used to charge the battery, and the other part is transmitted to the motor through the motor controller. The motor generates electromagnetic moment to drive the vehicle.

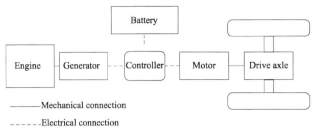

Fig. 7-6 Series hybrid power system

Parallel Hybrid Power System

The structure of parallel hybrid power system is shown in Fig. 7-7. Parallel Hybrid Power System has two sets of drive systems: internal combustion engine and motor. Internal combustion engines and motors can drive cars independently. When high power is needed, the car can also be driven by internal combustion engine and motor. The defect of insufficient maximum power of series hybrid power system is improved.

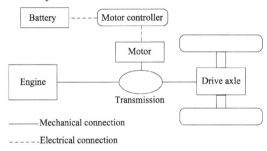

Fig. 7-7 Parallel hybrid power system

Hybrid Power System

Fig. 7-8 shows the structure of the hybrid power system. Its working principle is that part of the power generated by the engine is conveyed to the driving bridge through the maple drive device, while the other part is driven by the generator to generate electricity, and the power generated is conveyed to the motor or battery. The torque generated by the motor can also be transmitted to the driving axle through the power composite device. Flexible series or parallel operation mode is adopted according to driving conditions.

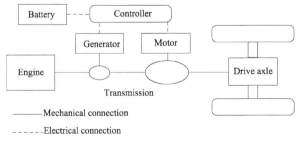

Fig. 7-8 Hybrid hybrid power system

At present, planetary gear mechanism is generally used as power compound device in the hybrid structure. For example, Toyota's Prius uses this structure, and its drive system is recognized as the most successful structure at present.

According to the ratio of battery-motor and internal combustion engine, it can also be divided into micro-mixed, light mixed fully mixed and externally rechargeable hybrid power system.

Passage 4 Working Process of Hybrid Electric Vehicle

As shown in Fig. 7-9, take an example of THS system to illustrate the working process of hybrid electric vehicle when it starts or runs under low load, runs at uniform speed, accelerates, stops or glides, brakes and decelerates.

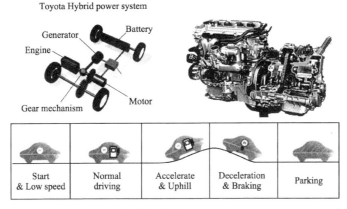

Fig. 7-9 Working process

1-Hybrid /ˈhaɪbrɪd/   混合动力
2-Power system /ˈpaʊə ˈsɪstəm/   动力系统
3-Generator /ˈdʒenəreɪtə(r)/   发电机
4-Engine   发动机
5-Gear mechanism /gɪə ˈmekənɪzəm/   齿轮机构
6-Motor   电机
7-Battery   电池
8-Start   起步
9-Low speed   低速
10-Normal /ˈnɔːml/ driving   正常行驶
11-Accelerate /əkˈseləreɪt/   加速
12-Uphill /ˌʌpˈhɪl/   爬坡
13-Deceleration /ˌdiːseləˈreɪʃn/   减速
14-Braking /ˈbreɪkɪŋ/   制动
15-Parking /ˈpɑːkɪŋ/   停车

Starting With Small Load

When the vehicle starts, runs at very low speed or on a steep slope, the engine will work in an inefficient area, so the control system will cut off the fuel and stop the engine. At this time, the fuel should be cut off according to whether the engine is idling or not, and the motor should be used to provide the output power to the vehicle. The path of the motor-driven vehicle is shown in path A in Fig. 7-10.

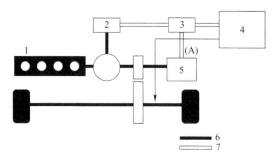

Fig. 7-10 Power transmission route of THS at start and small load

1-Engines;2-Generators;3-AC/DC converters;4-Batteries;5-Motors;6-Power transmission;7-Power transmission

Driving Normally

During normal driving, the engine power is divided into two output paths by the power distribution mechanism. One path directly drives the wheel (path B, Fig. 7-11), another path drives the generator to generate electricity, and uses the generated energy to drive motor 5, thereby increasing the driving force of the wheel (path C, Fig. 7-11). The relationship between the two power output paths is controlled by a computer to achieve optimal efficiency.

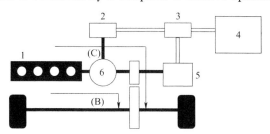

Fig. 7-11 Power transmission routes of THS during normal driving

1-Engine;2-Generator;3-AC/DC converter;4-Battery;5-Motor;6-Power distribution device

Full Load Acceleration

When full load accelerating, in addition to the power required in the above normal driving conditions, current should also be output from the battery, to increase the driving force of the wheel. The power of the vehicle comes from path A, B and C in Fig. 7-12.

Deceleration and Braking

When decelerating and braking, the wheel drives the motor. At this point, the motor becomes a generator, which uses the energy of deceleration or braking to regenerate power, and stores the recovered energy in the battery, as shown in Fig. 7-13.

Module 7 New Energy Vehicles

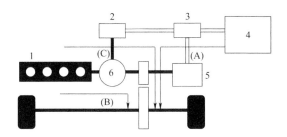

Fig. 7-12　Power transfer route of THS under full load acceleration

1-Engine；2-Generators；3-AC/DC converters；4-Battery；5-Motor；6-Power distribution device

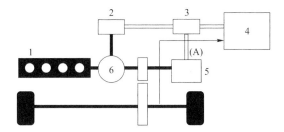

Fig. 7-13　Power transmission routes of THS during deceleration and braking

1-Engine；2-Generator；3-AC/DC converter；4-Battery；5-Motor；6-Power distribution device

Battery Charging

By controlling the battery, a certain charging state can be maintained. Therefore, when the battery charge decreases, the engine drives the generator to charge until it reaches the specified charging state, as shown in path D in Fig. 7-14.

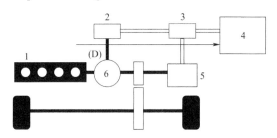

Fig. 7-14　Power transfer route of THS during battery charging

1-Engine；2-Generator；3-AC/DC Switch；4-Battery；5-Motor；6-Power distribution device

Parking

When the vehicle stops, the engine stops automatically. There is no idling like a conventional engine, no harmful substances and CO_2 emissions, but also save energy. When the battery does not reach the required charging state, even if it stops, the engine will drive the generator and charge the battery through path D. When the ignition power is switched on and the car has not yet started, the engine will automatically stop running after reaching the specified thermal state. If connected with the air conditioning switch, the engine will also run after parking.

Part II Skill Training

Circuit Identification

Reading Battery control circuit diagram of Toyota Prius hybrid electric vehicle, and answer the following two questions(Fig. 7-15).

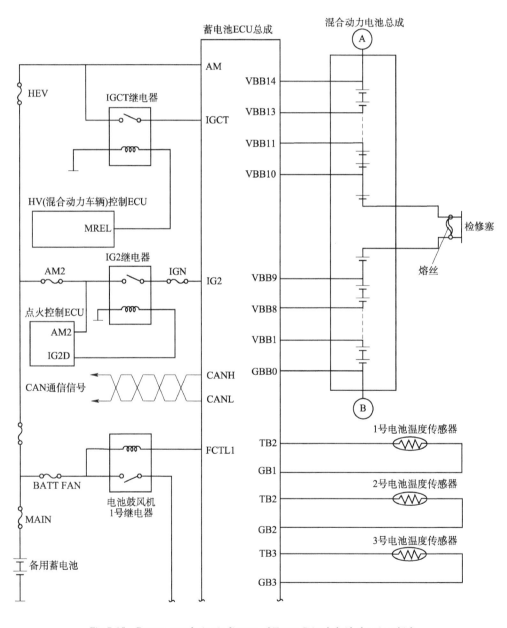

Fig. 7-15 Battery control circuit diagram of Toyota Prins hybrid electric vehicle

(1) What is the composition of battery control circuit for hybrid electric vehicle?
(2) What is the function of battery control circuit for hybrid electric vehicle?

Part Ⅲ　Exercises

Text Review

Exercise 1：Translate the following phrases into Chinese or English

1. 蓄电
2. _____　Hybrid Electric Vehicles
3. 电动机
4. _____　Pure Electric Vehicles
5. 再生制动系统
6. _____　DC/DC Converter
7. 充电站
8. _____　Direct-current dynamo
9. 爬坡
10. _____　AMT

Exercise 2：Mark the following statements with T(True) or F(False) according to the passage.

(　　)1. The working principle of pure electric vehicle is battery-current-power regulator-motor-vehicle driving.

(　　)2. Pure electric vehicles can be divided into lead-acid battery electric vehicles, nickel-hydrogen battery electric vehicles and lithiumion battery electric vehicles according to the types of batteries.

(　　)3. Hybrid electric vehicles have more advantages than pure electric vehicles in driving mile-age.

(　　)4. Hybrid electric vehicles have different power system configurations, which can be divided into series, parallel and hybrid.

(　　)5. When the hybrid electric vehicle accelerates at full load, it only needs the power required in normal driving conditions to meet the power demand.

Exercise 3：Translate the following paragraph into Chinese.

At present, the new energy vehicles are mainly natural gas vehicles, liquefied petroleum gas vehicles, electric vehicles, solar vehicles, fuel cell vehicles and hybrid electric vehicles. Pure electric vehicles are equipped with storage batteries, motors, motor control devices and energy management systems, and the way of energy supplement is changing.

Part Ⅳ   Listening and Speaking

Repair

Dialogue 1

A: Hi, I'm the mechanic. What can I do for you?

B: My car makes a very weird noise. It sounds like this: gulug, gulug, gulug...

A: Hmm, that doesn't sound good. Where does it come from?

B: I'm not sure. When I'm in the car, it sounds like coming from the engine, but when I get out of the car, it sounds like coming from directly under the trunk, maybe the muffler?

A: Maybe. How long is it since the noise came up?

B: About a week.

A: On what condition does the noise come up?

B: As long as the car is running.

A: What special event have your car ever undergone before the noise come up, say, crash? Or tune-up?

B: Nothing. But it is about the time to have it tuned up. It is already half a year since its last upkeep.

A: OK. I will take it down. I need to examine the engine.

B: OK. I will pop the hood up.

A: Hmm, your battery needs to be replaced. Would you please start your engine?

B: Sure.

A: There is an orderly noise. Is this the noise you've ever noticed?

B: Yes, that's it.

A: You need to replace your battery and give your car a tune-up. We will arrange a technician to make a full examination and see if anything more is wrong with your car. Is it all right for you?

B: That sounds nice. Thank you!

Dialogue 2

A: What can we do for you today?

B: Uh, hi. Yes, There is a problem with my car. It doesn't run. I mean every time I start it up, the engine runs for a minute or so, sputters like it doesn't get enough gas, and then dies.

A: Hmmm. Okay. Let's open the hood, and take a look... Okay, start it up.

Engine starting...

A: Okay, Okay. Shut her off. Hmmm. Let me look at the manual here... It sounds like a fuel line, a bad accelerator, a bad alternator, or even a weak battery possibly.

B: So, which one is it?

A: Uhh. Difficult to say. A further examination and test is necessary.

B: Okay, so how much is it going to cost?

A: Ah. Here, $200 for the pre-screening check, $150 for parts, plus or minus $100, and $75 an hour for labor. Oh, oh yeah. Today's a holiday, so labor is actually $50 more per hour.

B: Huh? Those prices are outrageous, and what holiday is it today?

A: Oh, it's the local pumpkin festival.

B: Ah, come on. I can't believe this. Of all my luck, my car broke down in a remote town, and it'll cost an arm and a leg to get my car fixed.

A: Ah, it happens so. You may watch the live broadcast of the festival on the TV set over there, and Mike, our technician will take care of your car. It may take an hour or so.

Module 8　Smart Vehicle

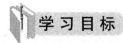

(1)能够用英语介绍车载网联的类型;
(2)能够用英语描述 CAN 总线的组成和作用;
(3)能够用英语介绍 CAN 总线的传递原理;
(4)能够用英语描述智能网联汽车的不同层级;
(5)能够用英语介绍智能网联汽车的关键技术。

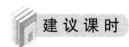

10 课时。

Part Ⅰ　Reading Materials

Passage 1　Types of Vehicle Network

　　Electronic technology in the field of automotive technology is developing rapidly. The increasingly complex and highly integrated automotive electrical appliances have made it necessary for automotive engineers to seek for faster and more efficient means of information transmission. The application of bus technology in vehicles makes more and more functions of the car possible. Fig. 8-1 shows the application of bus technology in automobiles The main bus types are shown in Fig. 8-2.

　　1-Camera /ˈkæmərə/　　　　　　　　　摄像头
　　2-Radar /ˈreɪdɑː(r)/　　　　　　　　　 雷达
　　3-Advanced /ədˈvɑːnst/ Driver Assistance
　　　 /əˈsɪstəns/ System (ADAS)　　　　　高级驾驶辅助系统
　　4-Gateway /ˈɡeɪtweɪ/　　　　　　　　　网关
　　5-Body control　　　　　　　　　　　　车身控制

Module 8　Smart Vehicle

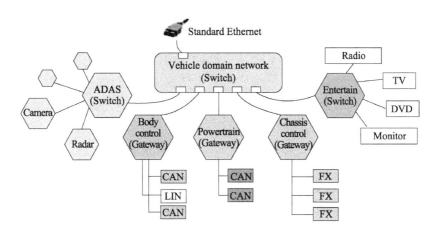

Fig. 8-1　Vehicle Network

6-Powertrain /ˈpauə trein/ 　　　　　　动力总成
7-Chassis /ˈʃæsi/ control 　　　　　　底盘控制
8-Controller Area Network (CAN) 　　控制器局域网络
9-Local Interconnect Network (LIN) 　本地互联网络
10-Entertainment /ˌentəˈteɪnmənt/ 　　娱乐
11-Monitor /ˈmɒnɪtə(r)/ 　　　　　　显示器
12-Television /ˈtelɪvɪʒn/ (TV) 　　　电视机
13-Radio /ˈreɪdiəʊ/ 　　　　　　　　收音机
14-Vehicle domain /dəˈmeɪn/ network 车域网
15-Standard Ethernet /ˈiːθənet/ 　　　标准以太网

Fig. 8-2　Bus types

CAN Bus

CAN is an abbreviation of Controller Area Network. CAN is an ISO international standardized serial communication protocol. In the automotive industry, a variety of electronic control systems have been developed for safety, comfort, convenience, low pollution, and low cost. A variety of electronic control systems have been developed, and the number of automotive wiring harnesses required for communication between these systems has also increased. In order to reduce the number of wire harnesses and the need for high-speed communication of large amounts of data, in 1986 German electrician Bosch developed a CAN communication protocol for automobiles. Since then, CAN has been standardized by ISO 11898 and ISO 11519, becoming the standard protocol for global automotive networks.

LIN Bus

The LIN bus is a low-cost serial communication network defined for automotive distributed electronic systems. It is a supplement to other automotive multiplex networks such as CAN. The LIN bus is suitable for applications that do not have high demands on the bandwidth, performance or fault tolerance of the network.

MOST Bus

The MOST bus was jointly developed by BMW, Daimler Chrysler, Harman/Becker (audio system manufacturer) and Oasis Silicon Systems. Designed to meet demanding automotive environments, the new fiber-based network is capable of supporting data rates of 24.8 Mbps, reducing weight and electromagnetic interference (EMI) compared to previous copper.

FlexRay Bus

FlexRay is a high-speed, deterministic, fault-tolerant bus technology for automobiles. It combines event triggering and time triggering, with efficient network utilization and system flexibility. FlexRay can be used as the backbone of a new generation of automotive interior networks.

Bluetooth

Bluetooth is a type of wireless network transmission technology originally used to replace infrared. Compared with infrared technology, Bluetooth can transmit data without alignment, and the transmission distance is about 0-20 meters (infrared transmission distance is within a few meters). With the help of signal amplifiers, the communication distance can reach up to 100 meters. Moreover, Bluetooth devices can also transmit sound, images, videos, etc., such as Bluetooth headsets.

Passage 2　CAN Bus

CAN is the abbreviation of Controller Area Network, which is the international standard serial communication protocol of ISO. The composition of the CAN bus includes: data bus, terminating resistor, transceiver, controller, node, gateway and so on. See Fig. 8-3.

Module 8 Smart Vehicle

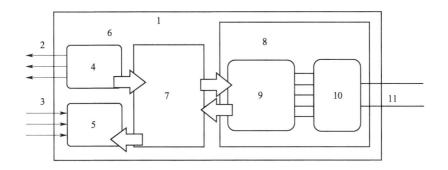

Fig. 8-3 CAN bus

1-Network node /ˈnetwəːk nəud/   网络节点
2-Executor /ɪɡˈzekjətə(r)/   执行器
3-Sensor /ˈsensə(r)/   传感器
4-Output /ˈautput/   输出
5-Input /ˈɪnput/   输入
6-Electronic /ɪˌlekˈtrɒnɪk/ Control Unit(ECU)   电子控制单元
7-Central Processing /ˈprəusesɪŋ/ Unit(CPU)   中央处理器
8-Interface circuit /ˈɪntəfeɪs ˈsəːkɪt/   接口电路
9-Protocol /ˈprəutəkɒl/ controller   协议控制器
10-Transceiver /trænˈsiːvə(r)/   收发器
11-CAN bus   CAN 总线

Data Bus

The data bus is the channel through which digital signals are transmitted between control units, the so-called information highway. The data bus in an in-vehicle network, similar to a network cable in a computer network. The data bus can realize that signals transmitted on a set of data lines can be shared by multiple control units at the same time, thereby maximizing the overall efficiency of the system and making full use of limited resources. See Fig. 8-4.

Fig. 8-4 Data bus

The CAN bus is divided into CAN high data line (CAN-H) and CAN low data line (CAN-L). Most of the cars use twisted-pair wired networks.

Terminating Resistor

The terminating resistor is the data transmission terminal of the network, and is usually a 120 Ω resistor. It is used to prevent data from being reflected back at the end of the transmission and generating reflected waves, because the reflected waves will destroy the data. See Fig. 8-5.

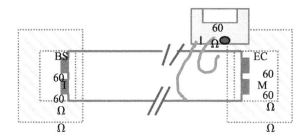

Fig. 8-5　Terminating resistor

Transceiver

A transceiver is a combination of a transmitter and a receiver. The function of the transmitter is to convert the data provided by the CAN controller into an electrical signal and send it out through the data line; the receiver is used to receive the data on the bus and transmit the data to the CAN controller.

Controller

The controller receives, processes, and transfers data between the CPU and the CAN transceiver. It receives the data sent by the CPU, processes and transmits it to the CAN transceiver. At the same time, it receives the data from the CAN transceiver, processes and transmits it to the CPU.

Node

When we use a computer to access the Internet and communicate with another computer in another place through a network, the computers at both ends are two nodes in the network, and the server terminal is also a node. In the CAN bus, the node is the control unit connected to the data bus. See Fig. 8-6.

Gateway

The main task of the gateway is to enable information exchange between two systems of different speeds. The gateway is equivalent to the train station in our life (Fig. 8-7). At station A, we arrived at a train (CAN drive data bus, 500 kBit/s) with hundreds of passengers. There is also a train on the station B (CAN Comfort / Infotainment data bus, 100 kBit/s) waiting, some passengers will change to this train, some passengers have to change to the express train to continue to travel. This function of the station, that is, the function of allowing passengers to change vehicles to reach their respective destinations through different speeds of vehicles, is the same as the gateway function of the CAN drive data bus and the CAN comfort/Infotainment data bus.

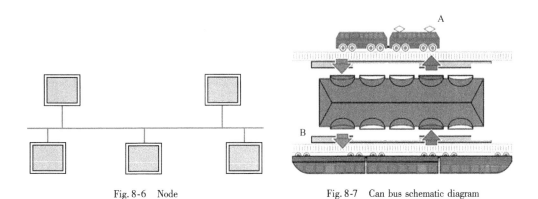

Fig. 8-6 Node   Fig. 8-7 Can bus schematic diagram

CAN Bus Data Transfer Process

(1) Provide data: The CPU in the node sends data to the CAN controller, and the CAN controller provides the CAN transceiver with data to be transmitted. See Fig. 8-8.

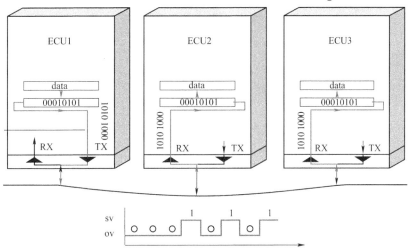

Fig. 8-8 Data transfer process

(2) Send data: All nodes are ready to broadcast data to the network, and the data of the node with the highest priority is sent.

(3) Receive data: All other nodes are converted to receivers and can receive data.

(4) Check data: The node receiving the data checks whether the received data is the data required by the node.

(5) Accept data: If the data is important to a node, it will be accepted and processed by the node, otherwise it will be ignored.

Passage 3 Overview of Smart Vehicle

The so-called "smart vehicle" is the addition of advanced sensors (radar, camera), controllers, actuators and other devices to the general vehicle (Fig. 8-9). Through the in-vehicle sensing system and information terminal, the intelligent information exchange with people, vehicles, roads, etc. is realized, so that the vehicle has intelligent environment sensing ability, can automatically analyze the safety and dangerous state of the vehicle, make the vehicle reach the purpose according to the will of the person, and ultimately achieve the purpose of replacing people to operate.

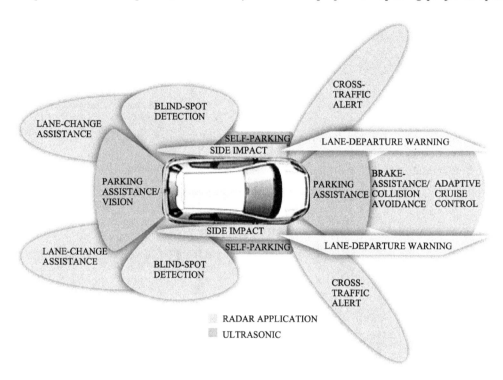

Fig. 8-9　Pilotless automobile

1-Pilotless automobile /ˈpailətlis ˈɔːtəməbiːl/　　无人驾驶汽车
2-Lane-change assistance /əˈsɪstəns/　　辅助变换车道
3-Parking assistance/vision /ˈvɪʒn/　　倒车雷达
4-Blind-spot detection /dɪˈtekʃn/　　盲点侦测
5-Side impact /ˈɪmpækt/　　侧面防撞
6-Self-parking　　自动泊车
7-Cross-traffic alert /əˈlɜːt/　　车侧警示
8-Lane-departure /dɪˈpɑːtʃə(r)/ warning　　偏离车道警报
9-Parking assistance　　停车辅助
10-Collision avoidance /kəˈlɪʒən əˈvɔɪdəns/　　防撞系统
11-Brake-assistance　　制动辅助
12-Adaptive /əˈdæptɪv/ cruise control(ACC)　　自适应巡航
13-Radar application /ˌæplɪˈkeɪʃn/　　雷达应用功能
14-Ultrasonic /ˌʌltrəˈsɒnɪk/ application　　超声应用功能

From a development perspective, smart cars will go through two phases. The first stage is the primary stage of smart cars, which is assisted driving; the second stage is the ultimate stage of smart car development, which is unmanned driving completely replacing human. The US Highway Safety Administration defines smart cars as the following five levels:

(1) No intelligence (Level 0): The driver always completely controls the original underlying structure of the car, including the brakes, steering gear, accelerator pedal and starter.

(2) Intelligence with special functions (Level 1): This level of car has one or more special automatic control functions. It can be called "assisted driving phase" by warning against car accidents. Many of the technologies at this stage are familiar, such as the Lane Departure Warning (LDW) System, the Frontal Collision Warning (FCW) System, and the Blind Spot Information System (BLIS).

(3) Intelligence with multiple functions (Level 2): This level of car has a system that combines at least two original control functions. There is no need for the driver to control these functions at all, which can be called "semi-automatic driving phase". The car at this stage will intelligently determine if the driver is responding to the dangerous situation of the warning. If not, it will take action for the driver, such as the Emergency Auto Brake (EAB) System and the Emergency Lane Assist (ELA) System.

(4) Unmanned driving with limited conditions (Level 3): This level of car allows the driver to completely control the car in a specific driving traffic environment. Moreover, the car can automatically detect changes in the environment to determine whether to return to the driver's driving mode, which can be called "high-automatic driving phase". Google driverless cars are basically at this level.

(5) Unmanned driving under full working conditions (Level 4): This level of car completely controls the vehicle automatically. The vehicle independently detects the traffic environment and can achieve all driving objectives. The driver only needs to provide a destination or enter navigation information, and does not need to control the vehicle at any time. It can be called "fully automatic driving phase" or "unmanned driving phase".

Passage 4　Key Technologies for Intelligent Networked Vehicles

The intelligent networked car is equipped with advanced sensors, controllers, actuators and other devices (Fig. 8-10). It integrates modern communication and network technology to realize intelligent information exchange and sharing between vehicles and X (people, cars, roads, backgrounds, etc.). It is a new generation of vehicles with complex environmental awareness, intelligent decision making, collaborative control and execution capabilities. In recent years, with the development of the automobile industry, the automobile has gradually turned to the transformation of "automation, intelligence, network, and sharing". Internet giants such as Google, Microsoft, Baidu, and other high-tech companies such as Tesla have entered the market. Intelligent networked cars have entered the stage of rapid development and become the hottest technology.

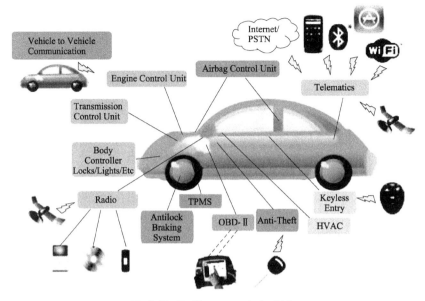

Fig. 8-10　Intelligent networked vehicle

1-Vehicle to Vehicle Communication /kəˌmjuːnɪˈkeɪʃn/ (V2V)　车辆与车辆通信
2-Airbag control unit　气囊控制单元
3-Engine control unit　发动机控制单元
4-Transmission /trænsˈmɪʃn/ control unit　传输控制单元
5-Body controller locks/lights/etc.　车身控制器锁/灯/等
6-Radio　收音机
7-Antilock braking system　防抱死制动系统
8-Tire Pressure Monitoring System (TPMS)　轮胎压力监测系统
9-On-Board Diagnostics /ˌdaɪəgˈnɒstɪks/ (OBD-II)　车载诊断技术(第二代)
10-Anti-Theft /θeft/　防盗
11-Heating, Ventilation /ˌventɪˈleɪʃn/ and Air-Conditioning (HVAC)　供热通风与空气调节
12-Keyless entry /ˈentri/　免钥匙进入
13-Telematics /ˌtelɪˈmætɪks/　远程信息处理
14-Public Switched /ˈswɪtʃt/ Telephone Network (PSTN)　公共交换电话网络
15-Wireless fidelity /fɪˈdeləti/ (Wi-Fi)　无线上网

Environment-Aware Technology

The mission of the environment-aware system is to use the main in-vehicle sensors such as cameras, radar, and ultrasound, as well as the V2X communication system to sense the surrounding environment(Fig. 8-11). By extracting road condition information and detecting obstacles, it provides decision-making basis for intelligent networked vehicles. Due to the complex driving environment of vehicles, current sensing technology cannot meet the needs of automatic driving development in terms of detection and recognition accuracy. However, deep learning has proved to have great advantages in complex environment perception. In the field of sensors, a variety of in-vehicle sensor fusion solutions have emerged to obtain rich peripheral environment information. High-precision maps and positioning are also important sources of environmental information for vehicles.

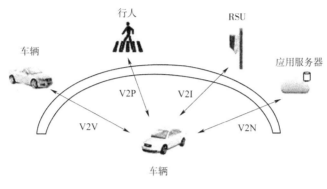

Fig. 8-11　V2X

Autonomous Decision-Making Technology

The decision-making mechanism should adapt to as many working conditions as possible under the premise of ensuring safety, and make correct decisions with comfort, energy saving and high efficiency. Commonly used decision methods include state machines, decision trees, deep learning, and enhanced learning. The state machine uses a directed graph to represent the decision mechanism and is highly readable. It can clearly express the logical relationship between states, but it needs manual design, and it is not easy to guarantee the performance when the state is complicated. Decision trees are a widely used classifier with a readable structure. It can be built by training the sample data, but has a tendency to over fit and requires extensive data training. The effect is similar to that of the state machine and is applied to automatic driving in some conditions. Deep learning and reinforcement learning can solve the complex working conditions through a large amount of learning in dealing with automatic driving decisions. Online learning optimization is also possible, but the performance of unknown conditions is not easy to determine.

Control Execution Technology

The task of the control system is to control the speed and direction of the vehicle so that it tracks the planned speed curve and path. Most of the existing automatic driving is for conventional working conditions, and more traditional control methods are used. Its reliable performance and high computational efficiency have been applied in active safety systems. In the field of control, a multi-agent system is a dynamic system formed by multiple agents with independent autonomy and interacting through certain information topologies. Using a multi-agent system approach to study vehicle queues can significantly reduce fuel consumption, improve traffic efficiency, and improve driving safety.

Communication and Platform Technology

The mode of vehicle communication can be divided into in-vehicle communication, inter-vehicle communication, and wide-area communication according to the coverage of communication. In-vehicle communication has evolved from Bluetooth technology to Wi-Fi technology and Ethernet communication technology. Inter-communication communications include dedicated short-range communication technologies and standards-based long-term communication technologies for shop floor communications. Wide area communication refers to communication methods such as 5G that are widely used in the field of mobile Internet. Through the networked wireless communication technology, the vehicle communication system integrates and analyzes the driver information, the vehicle information, and the environmental data surrounding the vehicle more efficiently. The vehicle transmits its location information and motion information to the cloud through communication between the vehicle and the cloud platform. The cloud controller combines road information and traffic information to optimize vehicle speed and gear to improve vehicle fuel economy and improve traffic efficiency.

Information Security Technology

Combined with the actual development of intelligent networked vehicles, the network management data object is determined and hierarchical management is implemented. Establish a data security system for data storage security, transmission security, and application security three-dimensionality. Data security technology framework is established including cloud security, line security, and end security, and develop intelligent network association data security technology standards. There are many innovative research directions around the surrounding industries in the field of information security technology. For example, in the aspect of information security testing and evaluation, the information security attack and research of smart cars is carried out by interfering with the vehicle's communication equipment and the on-board sensing devices such as radar and camera.

Part Ⅱ Skill Training

Circuit Identification

Read the model topology of Audi A6L (C7) (Fig. 8-12) and answer the following two questions.

(1) What types of CAN bus are available on the Audi A6L (C7)?

(2) What control modules are available on the Audi A6L (C7) MOST bus?

Module 8 Smart Vehicle

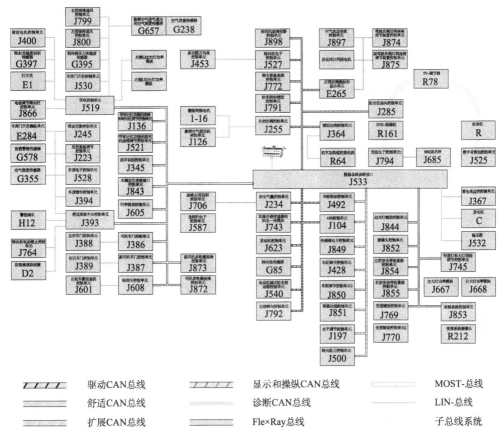

Fig. 8-12 Model topology of Audi A6L(C7).

Part Ⅲ Exercises

Text Review

Exercise 1: Translate the following phrases into Chinese or English.

1. _____   ADAS
2. 控制器局域网   _____
3. _____   Executor
4. 传感器   _____
5. _____   ECU
6. 收发器   _____
7. _____   Self-parking
8. 自适应巡航   _____
9. _____   V2V
10. 免钥匙进入   _____

Exercise 2: Mark the following statements with T(True) or F(False) according to the passage.

(   )1. FlexRay is a low-speed, deterministic, fault-tolerant bus technology for automobiles.

(   )2. The CAN bus is divided into CAN high data line (CAN-H) and CAN low data line (CAN-L), most of the cars used are twisted-pair wired networks.

(   )3. The terminating resistor is used to prevent data from being reflected back at the end of the transmission and generating reflected waves even though the reflected waves will not destroy the data.

(   )4. Unmanned driving under full working conditions (level 4) can be called "fully automatic driving phase" or "unmanned driving phase".

(   )5. The cloud controller combines road information and traffic information to optimize vehicle speed and gear to improve vehicle fuel economy and improve traffic efficiency.

Exercise 3: Translate the following paragraph into Chinese.

Each system actually includes some subdivided systems and functions. For example, the intelligent driving system is a big concept and one of the most complicated systems. It includes: intelligent sensing systems, intelligent computer systems, assisted driving systems, intelligent public transport systems, and so on. The life service system includes functions such as audio-visual entertainment, information inquiry and various biological services. For location service system, in addition to providing accurate vehicle positioning, it is also necessary to allow the car to communicate with other cars in an automatic position to achieve the intended purpose.

Part Ⅳ Listening and Speaking

Car Rental and Test Drive

Dialogue 1

A: How can I help you today?

B: I would like to rent a car.

A: Sure. We have several cars to choose from. What size are you looking for?

B: I'll take a midsize car.

A: How long will you be renting the car?

B: One week.

A: Would you like an insurance?

B: How much is it?

A: It is $14.95 a day and it covers everything regardless of fault.

B: Yes, please.

A: May I have your name?

Module 8 Smart Vehicle

B: My last name is King. K-I-N-G. My first name is Kerry. K-E-R-R-Y.

A: Your address, please?

B: I am from Canada. Do you need my address in Canada?

A: Just the city name.

B: Vancouver.

A: May I see your driver's license and your credit card?

B: Sure. Here they are

A: Great. That will be $324.92. Would you like me to charge it on this card?

B: Yes. That will be fine.

A: Please sign here. You can pick up your car downstairs. The expected time to return the car is June 29th. That is exactly one week from today. Show the attendant this invoice. When you return the car, bring this invoice with you. Is there anything else I can do for you?

B: That will be all. Thank you.

A: Thank you. Good bye.

Dialogue 2

A: What can I do for you?

B: Yes. May I take a test drive of the Honda Pilot?

A: Yes, but we'll have to undergo some procedures before you get the key. And is it the only car you'd like to try?

B: Yes. Actually I'm interested in both Pilot and Highlander. But I've driven the latter of my friend's.

A: Got it. Would you please show me your driver's license?

B: Sure. Here you are.

A: Thank you! I need your phone number too.

B: +86-591-88881234.

A: And your company and its address?

B: Rainbow International Trade Company at Building #1, High-Tech Zone, No. 80 Fortune Road, Happy Village, Fuzhou City, Fujian.

A: All right. One of our attendants, Jay Lee, will be with you in the car. Anything else can I do for you?

B: That will be all. Thank you!

A: Here is the key. Have a good ride!

B: Thanks!

附件1 参 考 译 文

模块一 汽车维修概述

文章1 乘用车的类型

随着汽车在日常生活中的日益普及化,人们对了解汽车各项相关专业知识的渴望也日益迫切。我们先来了解一下汽车的车身参数,如图1-1所示。

布局

这一节是对汽车的总体介绍。多年来,人们尝试了许多不同寻常的设计,有些比其他的更成功。最常见的当然是在矩形车厢的4个角各配上一个车轮!为了进一步理解这个相当简单的概念,我们可以用不同的方式对车辆进行分类。例如,按布局(图1-2~图1-5)分类如下:

(1)发动机前置前轮驱动;
(2)发动机前置后轮驱动;
(3)发动机前置四轮驱动;
(4)发动机后置后轮驱动;
(5)发动机中置后轮驱动;
(6)发动机中置四轮驱动。

以下段落和要点突出了上述车辆布局的特点。这些布局的常见缩写如表1-1所示。

常用缩写　　　　　　　　　　　　　　　　　表1-1

FWD	前轮驱动	AWD	全轮驱动
RWD	后轮驱动	4WD	四轮驱动

标准汽车的常见布局是发动机前置前轮驱动的汽车。这样的设计有很多优点:

(1)发生碰撞时,它为车辆前部提供保护;
(2)因为空气流动,发动机冷却更简单;
(3)如果质量集中是在前面,可以更好地转弯;
(4)发动机横向安装,更具备优势;
(5)乘客舱有更多的空间;
(6)动力装置可以作为一个完整的单元;
(7)驾驶行为引导车轮指向同一个方向。

过去的发动机后轮驱动是多年来使用的方法。一些制造商继续使用它,例如宝马。其主要的特点是长传动轴从变速器到最后的驱动,作为后桥的一部分传动轴有万向节,以允许悬架运动。这种布局有一些优势:

（1）当加速时质量转移到后驱动轮上；

（2）不需要像前轮驱动车辆那样复杂的等速万向节。

四轮驱动结合了上述所有优点，但使车辆更复杂，因此更昂贵。四轮驱动的主要不同之处在于需要一个额外的变速器，即传动箱来连接前轮和后轮驱动。

后置发动机的设计不是很受欢迎，但它被用于有史以来最畅销的汽车：大众甲壳虫。其优点是质量放在后轮，抓地力强，动力单元和驱动可以全部组装在一起。一个不利的方面是前面放行李的空间变小了。它的最大问题是操纵受到影响，因为转向盘的质量较小。平台式发动机是这类车辆最常见的选择。

将发动机安装在汽车的中间位置有一个主要缺点：它会占用车内更大空间。这使得它对于大多数"普通"车辆来说是不切实际的。然而它的质量分布非常好，这使得它成为高性能汽车设计师的选择。法拉利 Testarossa 就是一个很好的例子。"中置发动机"是用来描述发动机位于车轴之间的任何车辆，即使发动机不在车轴中间。

类型

轻型汽车的类型可以从小型双座跑车到大型载客汽车或运动型多功能车（SUV）。也包括轻型商用车，如轻型客车和皮卡车。很难对汽车进行准确地分类，因为在不同的国家有不同的系统。图 1-6 ~ 图 1-13 显示了一些不同的车身类型。

文章 2　主 要 系 统

无论我们如何对它们进行分类，所有的车辆设计都有相似的主要部件，而且这些部件的工作方式几乎相同。汽车的 4 个主要部分是车身、发动机、底盘和电气系统。其主要部件如图 1-14 所示。

发动机

该区域包括发动机本身以及燃料、点火、供气和排气系统（图 1-15）。在发动机中，燃料 - 空气混合物通过进气歧管进入，依次进入每个汽缸。由此产生的膨胀气体推动曲柄上的活塞和连杆，就像骑自行车人的腿推动踏板一样，从而使曲轴旋转。飞轮将每个活塞产生的动力平顺输出，动力通过曲轴末端的飞轮离开发动机进入离合器。废气通过排气系统排出。

底盘

这个区域由制动、转向和悬架系统以及车轮和轮胎组成。液压用手起动制动系统使车辆减速或停车。转动盘夹在摩擦衬里的衬垫之间（图 1-16）。采用机械连杆操纵驻车制动器。两个前轮是机械连接，必须一起转动，以提供转向控制。最常用的方法是使用齿条和小齿轮。转向盘与小齿轮相连，当小齿轮转动时，转向盘使齿条前后移动，齿条又使车轮转动。轮胎还能吸收一些路面振动，在路面保持中起着非常重要的作用。剩下的大部分冲击和振动都被驾驶员和乘客座位上的弹簧吸收了。弹簧可以是线圈式的，与阻尼器一起使用，以阻止它们产生振荡（上下跳动太多）。

在这个区域，离合器允许驾驶员将驱动器与发动机断开，使车辆改变静止状态。发动机飞轮与离合器盖螺栓紧固在一起，使离合器始终随发动机旋转。当离合器踏板抬起时，动力传递给变速器。变速器是必需的，因为发动机只有在快速转动时才能产生动力。变速器有助于驾驶员使发动机保持最佳转速。当变速器处于空挡位置时,动力不会消失。最后的驱动总成和差速器将驱动器连接到车轮、半轴或传动轴上(图1-17)。这种差速器允许传动轴和车轮在车辆转弯时以不同的速度旋转。

电气

电气系统包括照明设备、刮水器和仪表等。其中一个关键部件是交流发电机(图1-18),它由发动机驱动,产生电力来运行电力系统并给电池充电。起动电动机从电池中获取能量来起动发动机。电器元件由一系列开关控制。电子系统使用传感器来感知环境,驱动器来控制各种各样的部件——事实上,在现代汽车上几乎控制所有的部件。

文章3 车间安全

操作人员必须遵守有关安全操作规程的规定,以便将与汽车维修相关的对健康和安全的危害降到最低。对于熟练的、有经验的操作员来说,这并不意味着对他们的活动施加任何额外的限制,而仅仅表示他们在执行任务时应不断地考虑到自己及其同事的健康和安全。我们可以从干净、整洁的工装入手,如图1-19所示。

5S 理念

5S活动起源于日本,是一种优秀的现场管理技术。5S是保持车间环境,实现轻松、快捷和可靠(安全)工作的关键点。

如何确保汽车维修的质量?

(1)保持工作场地整洁、有序。

(2)尽力保持工作场地整洁,首先是不要弄脏它。

整理

目的:此过程将确定某种项目是否需要,不需要的项目应立即丢弃以便有效利用空间(图1-20)。

(1)按照必要性,组织和利用所有的资源,包括工具、零件或信息等。

(2)在工作场地指定一处地方来放置所有不必要的物品。

(3)收集工作场地中不必要的物品,然后合理合规地丢弃。

(4)丢弃不需要的物品。

整顿

目的:方便零件和工具的使用,节约时间(图1-21)。

(1)将很少使用的物品放在单独的地方。

(2)将偶尔使用的物品放在你的工作场地。

(3)将常用的物品放在你的身边。

清扫

目的:清除工作场所的脏污,使设备永远处于完全正常的状态,以便随时可以使用(图1-22)。

(1)一个肮脏的工作环境是缺少自信的表现。

(2)要养成保持工作场地清洁的好习惯。

清洁

目的:清洁是一个尽力保持整理、整顿和清扫状态的过程,防止任何可能问题的发生

(图1-23)。

(1)任何事情都要有助于使工作环境保持清洁,如颜色、形状以及各种物品的布局、照明、通风、陈列架和个人卫生(图1-24)。

(2)如果工作环境变得清新明亮,它能够给顾客带来良好的气氛。

自律

目的:自律是一个通过培训等使员工具有优良意识和习惯,然后成为优秀员工的过程。

(1)自律形成文化基础,这是确保与社会协调一致的最基本的要求。

(2)自律是学习规章制度方面的培训。通过这个培训,使学员学会尊重他人、使他人感到舒心。

文章4　正确使用工具

在车间工作时,我们会使用各种工具,如图1-25所示。同时,在使用的过程中,可能会遇到特殊危害,安全防范措施如下:

(1)进食、饮水或使用厕所设施前,应先洗手,以免把密封剂、颜料、溶剂、铁屑、铅及其他金属的残余物从双手转移到身体的内部及其他敏感部位。

(2)不要使用煤油、稀释剂或溶剂清洗皮肤。它们会去除皮肤的天然保护油,导致皮肤干燥和受刺激,或有严重的毒性作用。不要过度使用无水洗手液、肥皂或清洁剂,因为它们能去除皮肤的保护屏障油脂。经常使用隔离霜来保护双手,尤其是防止燃料、油、油脂、碳氢化合物溶剂和以溶剂为基础的密封剂对双手皮肤的伤害。一定要遵守工作规范,尽量减少液体或物质接触暴露皮肤以及停留在皮肤上的时间。用肥皂和水尽快彻底清洗皮肤上的污染物,如用过的机油。当没有肥皂和水时,可以使用无水洗手液。使用无水洗手液后,一定要涂上护肤霜。不要把污染的或油性的抹布放在口袋里或塞在腰带下面,因为这样会导致皮肤持续接触污染物。

(3)切勿将危险液体倾倒弃置在地面、排水渠或污水渠内。

(4)不要继续穿着已被严重污染或有酸、油、油脂、燃料或有毒溶剂溢出的工作服。严重污染工作服与皮肤长时间接触的后果可能是累积的,并可能危及生命。如果溶剂由于体温的影响而变得易燃,焊接或磨削产生的火花将穿戴者点燃,造成灾难性的后果。不要用气枪清洗有灰尘的工作服:它更容易把灰尘吹到皮肤上,可能会造成严重甚至致命的后果。再次穿受污染或油性衣物前,请务必清洗。一定要扔掉被污染的鞋子。只穿能给予足部足够保护的鞋,以防工具、尖锐或沉重的物体掉在鞋上。避免接触炽热或燃烧的物料。尖锐或发热的物体很容易穿透不合适的鞋子,如帆布鞋或运动鞋。鞋底也应保持良好的状态,以防止尖锐或热的金属片向上穿透。

(5)确保手套无孔,内部清洁。在处理危险或有毒物料时,应经常佩戴手套。

(6)保持护目镜清洁及保养良好。如有需要,请更换眼镜或护目镜。不要用有裂缝的眼镜。在使用台式磨床或便携式磨床、圆盘磨床、电锯和凿子时,一定要戴上护目镜。

(7)吸烟只能在吸烟区内进行。维修工作场所禁止吸烟。

(8)一辆正常行驶的汽车不需要经常充电,但是如果汽车经常行驶很短的距离或者长时间不行驶,电池就需要充电。充电时请将电池与车内电气系统断开。

(9)如果现场人员众多,灭火时一定要组织人员和附近车辆疏散。自救的时间一般在1分钟内。记住首先要用灭火器。火灾发生后几十秒内进行正确处理,对生命财产安全起着至关重要的作用。如果火势严重,据估计火势已失控,应组织疏散,并打119电话报火警。

(10)使用有故障和维护不善的电气设备或误用设备可能导致触电。所有电气设备必须经常检查并保持良好状态。弯头、电缆和插头不得以任何方式磨损、破裂、切割或损坏。设备必须有正确的额定熔断丝保护。尽可能使用低压设备。

(11)如何操作砂轮:

①不要戴手套;

②起动前检查砂轮是否松动;

③不要站在砂轮的前面;

④直到稳步轮旋转再开始研磨;

⑤不要碰撞砂轮;

⑥不使用普通的钳子夹紧小的工件。

(12)如何操作钻床:

①戴护目镜;

②不戴手套(特别是棉手套);

③修复钻头(直到它是同心的,不是偏心的);

④起动前检查砂轮是否松动;

⑤修复工件(用平钳夹小工件等);

⑥选择进给速度(慢下来时钻透);

⑦用扫帚清理铁屑(而不是吹)。

(13)铁屑进入眼睛的紧急处理:

①不要用手揉搓眼睛;

②不要用水冲洗眼睛;

③建议用软纸小心地将铁屑从眼睛上清除;

④如果有必要,请叫医生。

(14)如何使用手工工具:

①对于扳手来说,一般是拉而不是推。一定要小心推,以免伤到手。

②对于锤子来说,查看其是否变松。锤子末端不允许有毛刺。

(15)治疗烫伤:

①如果你被烫伤了,像往常一样用冷水给烫伤的皮肤降温。小心水可能渗进皮肤。建议在皮肤上涂抹特殊的烧伤膏。

②如果烫伤了,一定要尽快看医生。

模块二　汽车发动机

文章1　曲柄连杆机构

曲柄连杆机构是往复活塞式发动机将热能转换为机械能的主要机构,其功能是将燃气作用在活塞顶上的压力转变为曲轴旋转运动而对外输出动力。

曲柄连杆机构由活塞连杆组和曲轴飞轮组两部分组成。活塞连杆组包括活塞、活塞环、活塞销、连杆等零部件。曲轴飞轮组包括曲轴、飞轮、带轮、正时齿轮等零部件,如图 2-1 所示。

发动机工作过程中,燃料燃烧产生的气体压力直接作用在活塞顶上,推动活塞作往复直线运动。活塞作用力经活塞销、连杆传给曲轴,将活塞的往复运动转换为曲轴的旋转运动。发动机产生的动力大部分由曲轴后端的飞轮传给底盘的传动系统,再经过传动系统传给汽车的驱动轮;还有一部分动力通过曲轴前端的齿轮和带轮驱动发动机自身的其他机构和系统。

活塞

活塞的功能是与汽缸盖共同构成燃烧室,承受气体压力,并将此力通过活塞销传给连杆,以推动曲轴旋转。

活塞从构造上可分顶部、头部和裙部 3 部分。活塞顶部是燃烧室的组成部分,用来承受气体压力,汽油机活塞顶部形状与燃烧室形状和压缩比大小有关。活塞头部是活塞环槽以上的部分,其作用是:承受气体压力,并传给连杆;与活塞环一起实现汽缸的密封;将活塞顶所吸收的热量通过活塞环传导到汽缸壁上。活塞裙部是指油环槽下端以下部分,是用来为活塞运动导向和承受侧压力的。因而裙部要有一定的长度,以保证可靠的导向;此外,裙部应有足够的实际承压面积,以承受侧压力。

活塞环

活塞环是具有弹性的开口环,按其功能可分为气环和油环两类。气环又叫压缩环,其作用是保证活塞与汽缸壁间的密封,防止汽缸中的气体窜入曲轴箱;同时还将活塞头部的热量传给汽缸壁,再由冷却液或空气带走;另外还起刮油、布油等辅助作用。一般发动机上每个活塞装有 2～3 道气环。

油环用来刮除汽缸壁上多余的机油,并在汽缸壁上布上一层均匀的油膜,这样既可以防止机油窜入汽缸燃烧,又可以减小活塞、活塞环与汽缸的磨损和摩擦阻力。此外,油环也起到密封的辅助作用。通常发动机有 1～2 道油环。

活塞销

活塞销的功能是连接活塞和连杆小头,将活塞承受的气体压力传给连杆。

活塞销在高温下承受很大的周期性冲击载荷,润滑条件较差(一般靠飞溅润滑),因而要求活塞销具有足够的刚度和强度、表面耐磨、质量尽可能小。为此,活塞销通常做成空心圆柱体。

连杆

连杆的功能是将活塞承受的力传给曲轴,推动曲轴转动,从而使活塞的往复运动转变为曲轴的旋转运动。

连杆在工作时承受压缩、拉抻和弯曲等交变荷载。因此要求连杆在具有足够的刚度和强度的前提下质量应尽可能小。

曲轴

曲轴的主要功能是承受连杆传来的力,并由此产生绕自身轴线的旋转力矩,该力矩通过飞轮对外输出;另外,曲轴还用来驱动发动机的配气机构和发电机、水泵、转向油泵、空气压缩机等附件。

曲轴一般由前端、主轴颈、连杆轴颈、曲柄臂、平衡重和后端(动力输出端)等组成。曲轴前端轴用以安装水泵带轮、曲轴正时带轮(或正时齿轮、正时链轮)、起动爪等,曲轴后端凸缘用以安装飞轮。

飞轮

飞轮是一个转动惯量很大的圆盘,其主要功能是保证曲轴的旋转角速度和输出转矩尽可能均匀,使发动机运转平稳,并使发动机有可能克服短时间的超负荷。此外,飞轮又往往用作摩擦式离合器的主动件。同时,利用飞轮上的齿圈起动时传力。

文章 2 配气机构

配气机构的功能是按照发动机各缸的工作循环和做功次序,定时地将各个汽缸的进、排气门开启和关闭,以便使新鲜的可燃混合气(汽油机)或空气(柴油机)及时进入汽缸,并将各汽缸中燃烧后的废气及时排出。

配气机构由气门组和气门传动组两部分组成。气门组包括气门(进气门、排气门)、气门弹簧、气门座、气门导管等零部件。气门传动组包括凸轮轴、正时带轮(或齿轮、链轮)、正时带(或正时链条)、气门挺柱等零部件,如图 2-2 所示。

发动机工作过程中,曲轴正时带轮通过正时带驱动凸轮轴正时带轮转动,并通过气门挺柱驱动气门组件,利用凸轮轴上的凸轮的特殊形状和分布形式,适时准确地打开和关闭进、排气门,实现汽缸内气体顺利换气的目的。

气门

气门布置在汽缸盖上,用于开启或关闭各缸的进、排气口。位于进气口处的气门称为进气门,位于排气口处的气门称为排气门。

气门的工作条件非常恶劣。第一,气门直接与高温燃气接触,受热严重,散热困难,因而工作温度很高,排气门最高温度可达 600~800℃,进气门温度较低,但也达到 300~400℃;第二,气门承受气体力、气门弹簧力以及气门落座时的惯性冲击力;第三,气门的冷却和润滑条件较差。因此,要求气门必须具有足够的强度和刚度,并耐热、耐磨损和耐腐蚀。

气门座

汽缸盖上与气门锥面相结合的部位称气门座。气门座与气门头部一起对汽缸起密封作用,同时接受气门头部传来的热量,起到对气门散热的作用。

气门座的温度很高,又承受气门头部频率极高的冲击拍打作用,润滑条件又差,容易磨损。因此,铝汽缸盖和大多数铸铁汽缸盖均采用耐高温、耐磨损的材料制成的镶嵌式气门座圈。

气门导管

气门导管是汽缸盖内支撑气门的座孔,其功用是对气门的运动起导向作用,以保证气门作直线往复运动,使气门与气门座正确贴合。此外,还在气门杆与汽缸盖之间起导热作用。

气门杆与气门导管之间一般有 0.05~0.12mm 的间隙,使气门杆能在气门导管中自由运动。

气门弹簧

气门弹簧的作用是使气门自动复位关闭,保证气门与气门座紧密贴合,并使气门挺柱始终与凸轮表面接触而不相互脱离。

气门弹簧一般为等螺距圆柱形螺旋弹簧。气门弹簧下端支撑在汽缸盖的弹簧座内;而上端则压靠在气门杆端上的气门弹簧座上。

文章3 润 滑 系 统

润滑系统的功用

发动机工作时,很多零件都是在很小的间隙下与另一个零件做相对运动,如曲轴主轴颈与主轴承,连杆轴颈与连杆轴承,活塞、活塞环与汽缸壁,凸轮轴与凸轮轴轴承等。如果没有对这些零件表面进行润滑,必然会产生强烈的摩擦,加速磨损,最终导致发动机无法运转。因此,润滑系统是保证发动机能长期正常运转的重要系统。

润滑系统的功用是在发动机工作时连续不断地把数量足够、温度适当的洁净机油输送到全部运动件的摩擦表面,并在摩擦表面之间形成油膜,实现液体摩擦,从而减小摩擦阻力、降低功率消耗、减轻机件磨损,以达到提高发动机可靠性和耐久性的目的。机油循环的时候还可以对发动机部件进行冷却和清洁。

汽油机的润滑系统

汽油机润滑系统一般由机油泵、集滤器、机油滤清器、限压阀、旁通阀和机油管道等组成,有些汽油机润滑系统中还设有机油冷却器,如图2-3所示。

当发动机工作时,机油泵将油底壳中的机油经集滤器吸入。集滤器可防止大的机械杂质进入机油泵和润滑油路中。被机油泵压出的机油经机油滤清器过滤后流入缸体上的主油道中,并通过曲轴箱中的横向油道进入曲轴主轴颈,再通过曲轴中的斜向油道从主轴颈处流向连杆轴颈,进入连杆轴颈中的小部分机油通过连杆大头上的机油喷孔喷向活塞和汽缸壁,以润滑活塞和汽缸。另有一部分机油经缸体上的油道到达汽缸盖油道,进入凸轮轴轴承,润滑凸轮轴轴颈。此外,润滑油还经过相关的油道或喷嘴到达正时链条和正时链条自动张紧器(使用正时链条配气机构的发动机)、凸轮轴的凸轮表面、液力挺柱(使用液力挺柱的发动机)等,执行润滑任务或作为液压部件的工作介质。

文章4 冷 却 系 统

冷却系统的功用

冷却系统的功用就是使发动机尽快地达到正常的工作温度,并使发动机在工作过程中始终处于最佳的工作温度范围内。

发动机冷却要适度。若冷却不足,会使发动机过热,从而造成充气效率下降,早燃和爆燃倾向加大,致使发动机功率下降。过热还会使发动机运动零件间的间隙变小,导致零件不能正常运动,甚至卡死、损坏,或使零件因强度下降而导致变形和损坏。同时,过热还会使润滑油黏度减小,润滑油膜易破裂而使零件磨损加剧。也容易因为早燃而增加油耗。

若冷却过度,会使发动机过冷,导致进入汽缸的混合气体或空气温度低而难以点燃混合气,造成发动机功率下降、油耗上升。还会使润滑油黏度增大,造成润滑不良而加剧零件磨损。此外,因温度低而未汽化的燃油会冲刷汽缸、活塞等摩擦表面上的油膜,同时因混合气体与温度较低的汽缸壁接触,使其中原已汽化的燃油又重新凝结而流入曲轴箱内,不仅增加了油耗,而且使机油变稀而影响润滑,从而导致发动机功率下降、磨损加剧。

水冷式冷却系统

水冷式冷却系统是以水(或冷却液)为冷却介质,先将发动机受热零件的热量传给冷却液,再通过散热器散发到空气中去。采用水冷式冷却系统的发动机也称为水冷式发动机。其冷却系统由散热器、水泵、风扇、冷却液套和节温器等组成(图2-4),利用水泵强制冷却液在冷却系统中进行循环流动而达到散热的目的。

水冷式发动机的汽缸盖和汽缸体中都铸有相互连通的水套。在水泵的作用下,散热器内的冷却液被加压后通过汽缸体进水孔进入发动机,流经汽缸体及缸盖的水套而吸收热量,然后从汽缸盖的出水口沿水管流回散热器。由于汽车向前行驶及风扇的强力抽吸,空气由前向后高速通过散热器。因此,受热后的冷却液在流过散热器芯的过程中,热量不断地散发到大气中去,冷却后的液体流到散热器的底部,又被水泵抽出,再次压送到发动机的水套中,如此不断循环,把热量不断地送到大气中去,使发动机不断地得到冷却,从而保证发动机正常工作。

模块三 汽车底盘

文章1 离 合 器

离合器是汽车传动系统的组成部件之一,它通常装在发动机曲轴与飞轮的后端,用来分离或结合发动机和手动变速器之间的动力传递。

离合器的功能

(1)使发动机与传动系统逐渐接合,保证汽车起步平稳;
(2)中断动力传递,配合换挡,使换挡平顺;
(3)防止传动系统过载;
(4)提供临时空挡。

离合器的基本组成

离合器由主动部分、从动部分、压紧机构和分离操纵机构4部分组成,见图3-1。

主动部分

主动部分包括飞轮、离合器盖、压盘等部件。这部分与发动机曲轴连在一起。离合器盖

与飞轮靠螺栓连接,压盘与离合器盖之间靠3~4个传动片传递转矩

从动部分

离合器的从动部分即为从动盘,又称为离合器摩擦片。离合器正常接合时,从动盘两面的摩擦衬片分别与飞轮和压盘相接触,发动机的转矩即靠飞轮、压盘与从动盘接触面之间的摩擦作用而传到从动盘上。

膜片弹簧

压紧机构由若干根沿圆周均匀布置的压紧弹簧或一个膜片弹簧组成,它们装在压盘与离合器盖之间,用来将压盘和从动盘压向飞轮,使飞轮、从动盘和压盘三者压紧在一起。

分离操纵机构

分离操纵机构由离合器踏板、传动机构、分离叉、分离轴承套筒、分离轴承、分离杠杆、复位弹簧等组成

离合器的工作原理

1. 离合器的接合状态

离合器在接合状态下,压紧弹簧将飞轮、从动盘和压盘三者紧压在一起,发动机的转矩经过飞轮及压盘通过从动盘两摩擦面作用传递给从动盘,再由从动盘中间的花键毂传给变速器的输入轴。离合器所能传递的最大转矩的数值取决于摩擦面间的压紧力和摩擦系数,以及摩擦面的数目和尺寸。

2. 离合器的分离过程

欲使离合器分离,只需驾驶员踩下离合器踏板,分离套筒和分离轴承在分离叉的推动下,先消除分离轴承与分离杠杆之间的分离间隙,然后推动分离杠杆内端前移,使分离杠杆外端带动压盘克服弹簧作用力后移,此时从动盘与飞轮分离,摩擦力矩消失,从而中断了动力传递。

文章2　自动变速器

自动变速器是一种汽车变速器,它可以在车辆行驶时自动改变齿轮比,使驾驶员不必手动换挡。与汽车上的其他传动系统一样,它允许一个最适合以较高转速运行的内燃机在一定范围内提供车辆行驶所需的速度和转矩输出。

汽车中最常见的形式是液压自动变速器。该系统采用液力变矩器代替摩擦离合器,通过液压锁定和解锁行星齿轮系统来实现齿轮的更换。自动变速器的主要部件如图3-2所示。有些机器的速度范围有限或发动机转速固定,只使用转矩转换器向车轮提供一个发动机的可变转矩。

自动变速器用于汽车离合器的控制和变速的自动化。目前,自动变速器的自动换挡过程是由自动变速器的电控单元(ECU)控制的。

液力变矩器

变矩器由3部分组成:叶轮位于传动端,附着在壳体上,由发动机驱动;涡轮位于发动机一侧,由来自叶轮的流体驱动,驱动传动的输入轴;导轮改变液体流向,提高效率和加倍

转矩。

ATF 泵

当 ATF 泵旋转时,泵的部件在一个区域内分开时就会产生一个低压(真空),而大气压将迫使流体进入这个区域。当泵的部件一起移动时,压力就产生了。

行星轮系

由行星齿轮组以及离合器和制动带组成。这些机械系统提供不同的齿轮传动比,根据行星齿轮锁定的位置改变输出轴的转速。

为了使齿轮发生变化,两种离合器或制动带中的一种用来保持行星齿轮组中的某一特定部件不动,同时允许另一部件旋转,从而传递转矩并产生齿轮减速或超速比。这些离合器由阀体驱动,它们的顺序由变速器的内部程序控制。

液压操纵阀体

该控制电磁阀总成包括 4 个传动流体压力(TFP)开关、1 个线性压力控制电磁阀、4 个压力控制(PC)电磁阀、2 个位移电磁阀(SS)、1 个变矩器离合器(TCC)电磁阀、1 个传动流体温度(TFT)传感器和传动控制模块(TCM)。它还具有车辆线束连接器,连接到挡位开关及输入和输出速度传感器。

电子控制系统

自动变速器通过各种传感器将发动机转速、节流口、车速、发动机水温、ATF 油温等参数输入 ECU。ECU 根据这些信号进行分析、计算和处理,然后根据设定的位移规律,向位移电磁阀、油压电磁阀发出动作控制信号。换挡电磁阀与油压电磁阀将 ECU 动作控制信号转换为液压控制信号,控制阀板内各换挡执行机构的动作,从而实现自动换挡过程。

速度传感器

速度传感器由动力总成控制模块(PCM)或传动控制模块(TCM)来控制班次,并在两种速度与所要求的每个齿轮的预定比例不匹配时检测诸如打滑等故障。

变速杆

自动变速器的换挡控制机构为手动选择阀门的操作机构。驾驶员通过自动变速器手柄改变手动阀在阀板上的位置。控制系统采用自动液压控制原理或电子自动控制原理,根据手动阀的位置、节气门开度、车辆速度和控制开关的状态来控制换挡执行机构的操作按照一定的法律在齿轮传动,从而实现自动换挡。

文章 3 行 驶 系 统

驱动系统由车身(室)、车轴(转向驱动桥、驱动桥)、车轮(转向轮、驱动轮)、悬架(前悬架、后悬架)等总成组成,见图 3-3。

行驶系统用于将车辆的各种总成和部件集成到一个车身中,以支承整个车辆并保证行驶。

车身

现代轿车采用的是承载式车身,承载式车身是用车身兼做车架,汽车的所有零部件、总成都安装在车身上,车身要承受各种载荷的作用。因而这种车身成为承载式车身,广泛用于轿车和客车。

悬架

现代汽车的悬架虽有不同的结构形式,但一般都由弹性元件、减振器和横向稳定器等组成。

1. 弹性元件

汽车悬架中常用的弹性元件有钢板弹簧、螺旋弹簧、扭杆弹簧和油气体弹簧等。

2. 减振器

减振器用于衰减车身的振动,使振动的振幅迅速衰减,并保持车轮与地面间的接触,以提高汽车的乘坐舒适性和操纵稳定性。目前,汽车中广泛使用液压减振器。当车架与车桥作往复相对运动时,减振器中的油液反复流经活塞上的阀孔,阀孔的节流作用及油液分子间的内摩擦力便形成了衰减振动的阻尼,使振动的能量转变为热能,并由油液和减振器壳体吸收,然后散到大气中。

3. 横向稳定器

横向稳定器的作用是提高侧倾刚度,使汽车具有不足转向特性,改善汽车的操纵稳定性和行驶平顺性。当两侧悬架变形不等,车身相对路面发生倾斜,稳定杆扭转力矩起了阻碍悬架弹簧的变形,从而减小车身的侧倾和侧向角振动。

车桥

车桥通过悬架和车架(或承载式车身)相连,两端安装汽车车轮,其功能是传递车架(或承载式车身)与车轮之间各方向作用力及所产生的弯矩和转矩。

车轮

车轮用于安装轮胎,并承受轮胎与车桥之间的各种载荷的作用。

车轮是由轮毂、轮辋和轮辐组成的。轮毂通过圆锥滚子轴承装在车桥或转向节轴径上。轮辋用于安装和固定轮胎。轮辐用于将轮毂和轮辋连接起来。

为了保证汽车行驶的安全性,轿车、客车等车速较高的汽车车轮总成必须通过动平衡检测和调整后方可使用,这种车轮的轮辋边缘常常夹装有平衡块。

辐条式车轮由轮辋、衬块、螺栓、辐条、轮毂等组成。

文章4 制动系统

驻车制动器系统

驻车制动系统(图3-4)由手制动杆、驱动装置和驻车制动器组成。它是受机械控制的。当制动时,驾驶员通过拉索拉动手制动杆,使驻车制动器工作。停车制动可与行车制动一起起动。控制装置采用驻车制动索和后轮制动器中的驻车制动控制装置施加后轮制动器,起到驻车制动的作用。

鼓式制动器

图3-5所示是鼓式制动器的基本组成。车轮制动器的旋转部分是制动鼓8,它固定于轮

毂上并与车轮连接,与车轮一起旋转。固定部分是制动蹄10和制动底板11,其上面有两个支承销12,支承着两个弧形制动蹄10的下端。制动蹄外圆面上铆有摩擦片9,上端用复位弹簧拉紧抵靠在轮缸6内的活塞上。支承销和轮缸都固定在制动底板上,制动底板用螺钉与转向节凸缘(前桥)或桥壳凸缘(后桥)固定在一起。轮缸6用油管5与装在车架上的液压制动主缸4相通。主缸活塞3由驾驶员通过踩制动踏板1推动推杆2来操纵,制动蹄靠液压轮缸工作时张开而产生制动力矩。

盘式制动器

在钳盘式制动器中,固定的摩擦元件是位于制动盘两侧的一对或几对面积不大的带摩擦衬片的制动钳。钳盘式车轮制动器广泛地应用在轿车和轻型货车上。它的优点是散热良好、热衰退小、热稳定性好,最适于对制动性能要求较高的轿车前轮制动器,这是因为轿车前轮的制动力要求较高,后轮常选蹄鼓式制动器配合使用。

模块四 汽车电控

文章1 电控燃油喷射系统

汽油机电控燃油系统主要由油箱、油泵、燃油滤清器、燃油管路(进气管和回油管)、喷油器和燃油压力调节器组成,见图4-1。

燃料从油箱中抽出,由电动燃油泵加压至约350kPa。通过燃料过滤器去除杂质,加压的燃料流到位于发动机上方的燃料分配管。燃油分配管与安装在进气歧管中的燃油喷射器(喷油器)相连。喷油器是一种电磁阀,由发动机控制单元(ECU)控制。当通电时,喷油器打开。加压燃料被雾化并喷射到进气歧管中与那里的空气混合。在进气冲程中,混合物被引入汽缸。

电动燃油泵

叶片式电动燃油泵是一种常见的电动燃油泵。叶片式电动燃油泵壳体的一端为进油口,另一端为出油口。与进油口同侧的转子(叶轮)由位于泵壳中部的直流电机高速旋转。

当泵工作时,槽中的燃料随着转子高速旋转。由于离心力的作用,燃油出口的燃油压力增大。同时在进气道处产生一定的真空,使燃料通过进气道处的滤网流动并被吸收到燃油泵中,燃油泵经压缩后从电机周围的空间通过排气口泵出。

燃油滤清

燃油过滤器的作用是从燃油中去除污垢,因为污垢会堵塞喷油器。燃料过滤器安装在燃料输送管下游电动燃油泵,一般使用寿命超过40000km。

燃油分配管

燃油分配管用于将燃油以均匀、均压的方式输送到各汽缸的喷油器。它具有燃油和压力储存、避免燃油压力波动、保证向各种喷油器提供均衡燃油等作用。

喷油器

喷油器安装在进气歧管中,由 ECU 控制,喷油器的喷嘴朝向进气阀。在喷油器内部有一个通过线束连接到 ECM 的电磁阀。当电磁阀被 ECM 激活时,产生的磁力会吸附电枢和针阀。因此喷嘴是开着的。燃料通过针状柱塞与喷嘴之间的圆形间隙迅速从喷嘴中喷出。燃料被雾化后与空气混合。在进气冲程中,空气–燃料混合物被引入汽缸。

燃油压力调节器

燃油压力调节器一般安装在分配器燃油管的一端,其进油口与分配器燃油管相连,其底部的燃油出口与燃油回流管相连。上部的真空端通过软管连接到进气歧管。

采用燃油压力调节器调节燃油管道内的燃油压力,通过控制燃油喷射时间的长短,保证 ECM 能够准确控制燃油喷射量。

文章 2 电子点火系统

电控点火系统主要由各种蓄电池、点火控制器、点火线圈和火花塞等组成,见图 4-2。

电子控制点火系统通过各种传感器准确地获得各种操作参数的发动机,并通过电子控制精确控制点火提前角,使发动机的点火提前角在不同工况和条件下可以接近相应的最佳点火提前角。

蓄电池

电池和发电机(电池在起动时工作,发电机在起动后工作)为点火系统提供所需的电力。

点火线圈

其目的是将 12V 电源的低压转换为点火所需的 15~30kV 的高压。

根据所使用的磁路类型,点火线圈可分为开路点火线圈和闭路点火线圈两种。

火花塞

火花塞的作用是将高压电引入汽缸的燃烧室,产生火花点燃混合物。

火花塞由接线螺母(连接高压电缆)、绝缘子、中心电极、密封垫片、壳体、侧电极等组成。

点火控制器

点火控制器包括断电器、分电器、电容器和点火提前机构。断电器用于起动/关闭点火线圈的一次回路;分电器包括分电器盖和分电器头。

它用于将点火线圈产生的高压按各汽缸的工作顺序发送到各汽缸的火花塞上。

文章 3 防抱死制动系统

ABS 是在传统制动系统的基础上增加的一套控制系统,防止制动时车轮抱死。主要由轮速传感器、ABS 执行机构、ABS 电控单元和 ABS 警示灯组成,见图 4-3。

制动灯开关安装在制动踏板旁边,当驾驶员踩下制动踏板时,制动灯开关接通,将制动信号输入 ABS ECU,同时接通轿车尾部的制动灯电路。

每个车轮上安置一个轮速传感器,它们将各车轮的转速信号及时地输入到电子控制单元(ECU);电子控制单元是 ABS 的控制中心,它根据各个车轮轮速传感器输入的信号对各个车轮的运动状态进行监测和判断,并形成响应的控制指令,再适时发出控制指令给制动压力调节器;制动压力调节器是 ABS 中的执行器,它是由调压电磁阀总成、电动油泵总成和储液器等组成的一个独立装置,并通过制动管路与制动主缸(总泵,下同)和各制动轮缸(分泵,下同)相连,制动压力调节器受电子控制单元的控制,对各制动轮缸的制动压力进行调节,在不同路面附着情况下,每秒进行 4~10 个调节循环,在制动过程中用来确保车轮始终不抱死,车轮滑动率处于合理范围内。警示装置包括仪表板上的制动警告灯和 ABS 警告灯。

轮速传感器

车轮速度传感器的作用:检测车轮速度和速度信号输入到 ECU,适合滑移率控制方法。目前 ABS 系统中使用的轮速传感器主要有电磁型和霍尔型。

制动压力调节器

制动压力调节器根据 ABS 电控单元指令,通过电磁阀自动调节车轮制动器的制动压力。根据制动系统的不同,制动压力调节器可分为液压制动压力调节器和气动制动压力调节器。

ABS 电控单元

电子控制单元是 ABS 的控制中心,它的主要作用是接收传感器的信号并进行处理,判断车轮是否抱死,然后向制动压力调节器发出制动压力调节控制指令。

ECU 一般由传感器输入放大电路、运算修正电路、输出控制电路和安全保护电路 4 个基本电路组成。

文章 4　电动助力转向

如图 4-4 所示,电动式 EPS 是利用直流电动机作为动力源,电子控制单元 ECU 根据力矩传感器和车速等传感器提供的信号,控制电动机转矩的大小和方向。电动机的转矩在电磁离合器的作用下通过减速机构减速增加转矩后,加在汽车的转向机构上,使之得到一个与工况相适应的转向作用力。

其控制原理是当车速较低时,所需转向力较小,车速较高时,转向所需转向力适当增大。

转向器

其功能是增大由转向盘传到转向节的力,并改变力的传递方向。

它被用于将转向盘的旋转运动变成转向摇臂的摆动或齿条轴的直线往复运动来控制转向盘的摆动。

EPS ECU

EPS ECU 是电子助力转向系统的核心部件,主要用于接收各种传感器的数据,并根据各个数据控制助力电机的工作,以达到助力的效果。

转角传感器

转向盘角度传感器是 EPS 的一个组成部分,主要安装在转向盘的柱下方向。主要测量汽车转弯时转向盘的"转角"。

转向力矩传感器

通过计算驾驶员施加在转矩传感器上的转矩来计算转向动力力矩，从而达到转向动力的效果。

转向直流电机

EPS系统可根据动力电机的安装位置分为转向轴助力器、齿轮助力器和齿条助力器。转向轴助力 EPS 电机固定在转向轴的一侧，通过减速机构与转向轴连接，直接驱动转向轴助力转向。齿轮辅助 EPS 电机和减速机构与小齿轮连接，直接驱动齿轮辅助转向。机架 EPS 电机和减速机构直接驱动机架提供动力。

模块五　汽车电器

文章1　起动系统

要使发动机由静止状态过渡到工作状态，必须用外力转动发动机的曲轴，使汽缸内吸入（或形成）可燃混合气并燃烧膨胀，工作循环才能自动进行。曲轴在外力作用下开始转动到发动机开始自动地怠速运转的全过程，称为发动机的起动，这也是起动系的作用。

要使发动机起动，应满足一定的要求，除了对汽缸压缩压力、混合气浓度、电火花强度（汽油机）或着火温度（柴油机）的要求外，还要求起动系能为发动机提供起动转矩和起动转速。

如图5-1所示，当起动时点火开关转至ST挡，接通起动继电器线圈，使起动继电器触点闭合，通过50端子接通起动机电磁开关，电磁开关将30端子和C端子连接，也就是将蓄电池的电缆和起动机中的电动机连接，使起动机内部的电动机转动，带动发动机旋转起动。

蓄电池

蓄电池提供起动器所需的大电流。

起动系

电力起动系由起动机和控制电路两大部分组成。主要包括：蓄电池、起动机、起动继电器和点火开关（柴油机则称为起动开关）组成。对于具体汽车来说，可能还由起动安全开关（或起动安全继电器）、起动切断继电器等组成。

起动机的作用是将蓄电池提供的电力转化成起动力矩，通过小齿轮驱动发动机飞轮转动，使发动机起动。

起动机由直流电机、传动机构和控制装置组成。

直流电动机由电枢（转子）、磁极（定子）、换向器和电刷等主要部件构成。

电枢

直流电动机的转动部分称为电枢，又称转子。转子由外圆带槽的硅钢片叠成的铁芯、电枢绕组线圈、电枢轴和换向器组成。

定子

磁极在起动机中又称为定子,由固定在机壳内的定子铁芯和定子绕组线圈组成。定子铁芯由低碳钢制成、用螺母固定在起动机机壳上。定子铁芯上面绕有定子绕组线圈(又称励磁绕组),通电后产生磁极。直流永磁式电动机的定子铁芯是由永久磁铁制成,没有定子绕组线圈。

电刷与电刷架

电刷架一般为框式结构。其中正极电刷架绝缘地固定在端盖上,负极电刷架与端盖直接相连并搭铁。电刷置于电刷架中,电刷由铜粉与石墨粉压制而成,呈棕黑色。电刷架上有较强弹性的盘形弹簧将电刷压向换向器。

文章2 电动刮水器

风窗刮水器的作用是用来清除风窗玻璃上的雨水、雪或尘土,以保证驾驶员良好的视线。

风窗刮水器包括2个前风窗刮水器和1个后风窗刮水器之分。电动刮水器主要由直流电动机、涡轮蜗杆减速器、曲柄摇杆机构(曲柄、连杆、摆杆和机架)刮水器臂、刮水片架和刮水片等组成,见图5-2。

一般来说,电机和蜗壳集成在一起作为刮水电机总成。曲柄和曲柄摇杆机构将蜗杆的转动转化为摆臂的摆摆运动,使摆臂上的刮水片能够进行刮拭。

刮水电动机

刮水电动机有绕线式和永磁式两种。永磁式刮水电动机体积小、质量轻、结构简单,使用广泛。

永磁式刮水电动机主要由外壳、永久磁铁、电枢、电刷安装板、复位开关(铜环和触点)、蜗杆及蜗轮等组成。

电动机电枢通电即开始转动,以蜗杆驱动蜗轮,蜗轮带动曲柄旋转,曲柄通过连杆带动刮水片左右摆动。

刮水器速度偏慢的故障诊断

若刮水器各挡位的速度均比正常慢,应首先检查刮水电动机电源线路上的电压是否正常,若电压偏低,则应检查刮水器电路中的中间继电器、熔断丝、控制开关等部件上的接线端子插接是否牢固、部件工作是否正常。若电压正常,则应检查刮水电动机上的电刷接与换向器间接触是否良好、电动机轴承及蜗轮润滑是否良好。

文章3 灯光系统

为保证汽车行驶的安全性,提高车辆的利用率,减少交通事故和机械事故的发生,汽车上都装有多种照明设备和灯光信号系统,俗称"灯系"。

汽车照明系统主要用于汽车在夜间行车时照明道路、标示车宽度、车内照明、查看仪表和夜间检修等。照明系由电源、照明装置和控制部分组成。控制部分包括各种灯光开关和继电器等。照明装置包括外部灯、内部灯和工作照明灯。

外部灯

外部灯包括：车辆前面的前照灯、前示宽灯、前转向信号灯、前雾灯等。现在汽车基本都是使用组合式灯。车辆后面的有倒车灯、牌照灯、后示宽灯、制动信号灯、前转向信号灯和后雾灯等，见图5-3。

前照灯

由于它是汽车上面最大的灯，又称"大灯"，前照灯装在汽车头部的两侧，用于夜间或光线昏暗路面上汽车行驶时的照明。

超车灯

超车灯没有专业的灯泡，基本所有的汽车是在前照灯电路里面的变光开关里面设置了超车灯开关，当手拉变光开关到最高位置时超车灯开关接通远光灯亮、手一松开远光灯暗。

前示宽灯

它又称"小灯"，灯光颜色白色。用于夜间给其他车辆提示车辆位置与宽度。同时可以照亮车轮周围的路面。

后示宽灯

它又称"尾灯"，灯光颜色红色。用于夜间向其他车辆提示车辆位置与宽度。对于一些大型客车还有高位示宽灯和侧面示宽灯。

前雾灯

它安装在车头，位置比前照照灯稍低。前雾灯用于在有雾、下雪、暴雨或尘埃等恶劣条件下改善道路照明情况。

后雾灯

后雾灯是安装在车后发光强度比尾灯更大的红色信号灯。其作用是在雾、雪、雨或尘埃弥漫等能见度较低的环境中，为使车辆后方其他道路交通参与者指示车辆的宽度和位置。

转向信号灯

转向信号灯可分为前/后转向信号灯和左/右转向信号灯。其分别安装在车辆两端及前翼子板上，灯光颜色为黄色。点亮转向信号灯时向前后左右车辆表明驾驶员正在转向或将要改换车道的方向。

危险警告灯

车辆上面没有专用的危险警告灯，是在车辆灯光电路里面设置了危险警报灯开关。在开关接通时控制所有的转向指示灯亮。

制动灯

它安装在车辆尾部，颜色为红色。制动时点亮制动灯通知后面的车辆本车正在制动，以免后面的车辆与其后部碰撞。

牌照灯

牌照灯位于尾部牌照的上方，用于照亮车牌。当后示宽灯亮时，牌照灯也亮。

倒车灯

它安装于车辆尾部，当点火开关接通，变速杆换至倒车挡时，倒车灯亮。给驾驶员提供额外照明，使其能在夜间倒车时看清车辆后面，也警告后面的车辆，本车驾驶员想要倒车或正在倒车。

仪表灯

它用于夜间照亮仪表盘，使驾驶员能迅速看清仪表。示宽灯亮时，仪表灯同时亮。

顶灯

它用于车内乘客照明，但必须不致使驾驶员眩目。通常客车车内灯均位于驾驶室中部，使车内灯光分布均匀。

工作照明灯

工作照明灯包括：行李舱灯、发动机罩灯等。还有仪表盘上的各种指示灯和警告灯。

文章4　转向信号灯

汽车转向灯主要是用来指示车辆的转弯方向，以引起交通警察、行人和其他驾驶员的注意，提高车辆行驶的安全性。另外，汽车转向灯同时闪烁还用作指示危险警报。汽车转向灯的闪烁是通过闪光器来实现的，闪光器通常按结构和工作原理的不同分为电热丝式、电容式、晶体管式、集成电路式等。

以丰田花冠转向灯和危险警报灯电路为例，如图5-4所示。电路主要由蓄电池、点火开关、继电器、转向信号闪光器、转向灯开关、危险警报灯开关、防盗ECU和左右转向灯等组成。当打开点火开关时，蓄电池正极通过继电器的触点和转向信号闪光器的IG端子给转向信号闪光器的内部电子元件供电、通过端子GND搭铁回到蓄电池负极。

这时如果转向灯开关拨到左转向位置，给转向信号闪光器端子EL一个搭铁的低电压信号。转向信号闪光器接到信号后通过内部的电子元件将端子IG和端子LL接通。

左转向灯和左转向信号指示灯的电流路径是：蓄电池正极→熔断线→继电器触点→转向灯闪光器的端子IG→转向灯闪光器的端子LL→左前、左后和左侧三个转向灯和仪表盘上左转向灯信号灯共4个灯→搭铁→蓄电池负极。右转向灯工作过程基本相同。

危险警报灯工作原理如下：不管点火开关是否接通，只要闭合危险警报灯给转向信号闪光器端子EHW一个搭铁的低电压信号，转向信号闪光器接到信号后通过内部的电子元件将端子+B分别与端子LR和端子LL接通。

这时危险警报灯的电流路径是：蓄电池正极→熔断器→转向灯闪光器的端子+B→转向灯闪光器的端子LL和转向灯闪光器的端子LR→前/后、左/右和侧面转向灯和仪表盘上左/右转向灯信号灯共8个灯→搭铁→蓄电池负极。前/后、左/右和侧面转向灯的6个转向灯闪烁，利用全部转向灯闪烁起到危险警报灯的作用。

同时仪表盘上面的左/右转向灯信号灯也同步闪烁,提示驾驶员危险警报灯打开。

模块六　汽车安全与舒适

文章1　辅助约束系统SRS

辅助约束系统(SRS)功能

辅助约束系统为保护乘客,在汽车发生碰撞时瞬间打开,吸收及减轻冲击力所造成的伤害。

辅助约束系统工作原理

SRS主要组成如图6-1所示。SRS辅助约束系统在汽车发生碰撞时,可瞬间将安全气囊打开,与安全带一起对驾驶员及同乘辆车乘员提供保护,因此能有效减轻对头部及胸部造成的冲击。另外,在发生侧面碰撞时,SRS侧面安全气囊系统可保护坐在驾驶座及副驾驶座上乘客的胸部,SRS窗帘式安全气囊系统可保护坐在前后排座椅上乘客的头部。

辅助约束系统特点

(1)只有点火开关在ON或START位置时辅助气囊才能工作。点火钥匙转至ON位置后,辅助气囊警告灯点亮。如果系统能工作,辅助气囊警告灯将在约7秒后关闭。

(2)发生侧面碰撞时,可减轻对头部、面部及颈部的冲击。SRS窗帘式安全气囊在受到侧面冲击时,可瞬间打开安装在车顶侧面的安全气囊,有效保护前后排乘客。安全气囊在减缓因碰撞导致汽车台柱及玻璃对乘客头部、面部造成冲击的同时,还可抑制脖子过度弯曲及减轻颈部受到的伤害。

(3)在发生侧面冲撞、后方冲撞、翻车或严重程度较低正面碰撞时,辅助前气囊通常不会充气,要始终佩戴安全带以降低在各种事故中受伤的风险或严重性。

(4)在前排乘员安全气囊指示灯点亮或前排乘员座椅上没人的情况下,前排乘员安全气囊不会充气。除此之外,由于气囊系统存在一定危险性,一旦需要正确使用才能发挥SRS系统作用,因此对于配备SRS气囊车辆,在日常使用时,需要注意些事项。应确保正确驾驶姿势,并系上安全带,以确保驾驶员和乘员安全。

文章2　防盗系统

汽车防盗系统功能

汽车防盗器就是一种安装在车上,用来增加盗车难度、延长盗车时间的装置。如图6-2所示,它通过将防盗器与汽车电路配接在一起,从而可以达到防止车辆被盗、被侵犯、保护汽车并实现防盗器各种功能的目的。

汽车防盗系统类型

随着科学技术的进步,为对付不断升级的盗车手段,人们研制出各种方式、不同结构的防盗器。防盗器按其结构可分为4类:机械式、芯片式、电子式和网络式。

机械式防盗系统

机械式防盗装置是市面上最简单最廉价的一种防盗器,其原理也很简单。它只是将转向盘和控制踏板或挡柄锁住。其优点是价格便宜,安装简便;缺点是防盗不彻底,每次拆装麻烦,不用时还要找位置存放。

芯片式防盗系统

芯片式防盗的基本原理是锁住汽车的发动机、电路和油路,在没有芯片钥匙的情况下无法起动车辆。数字化的密码重码率极低,而且要用密码钥匙接触车上的密码锁才能开锁,杜绝了被扫描的可能。

芯片式防盗已经发展到第四代,具有特殊的诊断功能,即已获授权者在读取钥匙保密信息时,能够得到该防盗系统的历史信息。系统中经授权的备用钥匙数目、时间印记以及其他背景信息,成为收发器安全性的组成部分。独特的射频识别技术可以保证系统在任何情况下都能正确地识别驾驶者,在驾驶员接近或远离车辆时可以自动识别其身份,自动打开或关闭车锁。

电子式防盗系统

电子防盗就是给车锁加上电子识别,开锁配钥匙都需要输入十几位密码的汽车防盗方式。它一般具有遥控技术。它有如下4种功能。

1. 防盗报警功能

这个功能是指在车主遥控锁门后,报警器即进入警戒状态,此时如有人撬门或用钥匙开门,会立即引起防盗器鸣叫报警。

2. 车门未关安全提示功能

汽车熄火遥控锁门后,若车门未关妥,车灯会不停闪烁,喇叭鸣叫,直至车门关好为止。

3. 寻车功能

车主用遥控器寻车时,喇叭断续鸣叫,同时伴有车灯闪烁提示。

4. 遥控中央门锁

当遥控器发射正确信号时,中央门锁自动开启或关闭。

GPS 式的防盗系统

GPS 的工作原理是利用接收卫星发射信号与地面监控设备和 GPS 信号接收机组成全球定位系统。卫星星座连续不断发送动态目标的三维位置、速度和时间信息,保证车辆在地球上的任何地点、任何时刻都至少能收到卫星发出的信号。GPS 主要是靠锁定点火或起动来达到防盗的目的,同时还可通过 GPS 卫星定位系统,将报警处和报警车辆所在位置无声地传送到报警中心。

文章 3 空 调 系 统

世界上的制冷系统有许多类型,其中,最常用的是使用在小轿车上的膨胀阀式制冷系统,膨胀阀式制冷系统主要部件有压缩机、冷凝器、储液干燥器、膨胀阀和蒸发器5个部分,见图6-3。

空调系统的功能

(1)调节车内温度;

(2)调节车内湿度;

(3)调节车内空气流速;

(4)过滤和净化车内空气。

压缩机

压缩机是制冷系统的核心部件,其作用是借助外力维持制冷剂在制冷系统内的循环,吸入来自蒸发器的低温、低压的气态制冷剂,压缩气态制冷剂使其温度和压力升高,并将气态制冷剂送往冷凝器,在热量吸收和释放的过程中实现热交换。

冷凝器

为了更好地散热,冷凝器安装在进气格栅后部、发动机散热器的前面。冷凝器的作用是将压缩机排出的高温高压气态制冷剂与冷凝器外部的空气进行热交换,转变为高温高压的液态制冷剂,并把热量散发到车外环境中。

储液干燥器

储液干燥器用于膨胀阀式制冷系统中。其主要作用是:暂时存储制冷剂,使制冷剂的流量与制冷负荷相适应;滤除制冷剂中的杂质,吸收制冷剂中的水分,防止制冷系统管路脏堵和冰塞,保护设备部件不受侵蚀。

膨胀阀

膨胀阀是汽车空调系统中的一个重要部件,一般安装于储液干燥器和蒸发器之间。膨胀阀使中温高压的液态制冷剂通过其节流成为气态混合的制冷剂,然后制冷剂在蒸发器中吸热量达到制冷效果。膨胀阀通过蒸发器末端过地度变化来控制阀门流量,防止出现蒸发面积利用不足和"敲缸"现象。

蒸发器

制冷系统工作时,高压液态制冷剂通过膨胀阀膨胀而压力降低,变成湿蒸汽进入蒸发器芯管,吸收散热片及周围空气的热量。蒸发器通常装在仪表板后的风箱内,依靠鼓风机使车外空气或车内空气流经蒸发器,以便冷却与除湿。

汽车空调制冷系统工作原理

1. 压缩过程

压缩机将蒸发器低压侧的低温低压(温度约为 0℃、压力约为 0.15MPa)的气态制冷剂压缩成高温高压(温度约为 110℃、压力约为 1.5MPa)的气态制冷剂,送往冷凝器冷却降温。

2. 冷凝过程

送往冷凝器的高温高压气态制冷剂,在温度高于外部温度很多时,向外散热进行热交换,制冷剂被冷凝成中温高压(温度约为 60℃、压力为 1.0~1.2MPa)的液态制冷剂。

3. 膨胀过程

冷凝后的液态制冷剂经过膨胀阀使制冷剂空间体积增大,其温度和压力急剧下降,变为低温低压的气、液态混合的制冷剂,以便进入蒸发器中迅速吸热蒸发。在膨胀过程中同时进行流量控制,以便供给蒸发器所需的制冷剂,从而达到控制温度的目的。

4. 蒸发过程

气、液态混合的制冷剂经蒸发器不断吸热汽化转变成低温低压(温度约为 0℃、压力约为 0.15MPa)的气态制冷剂,吸收车内空气的热量。

文章 4　导 航 系 统

汽车导航系统由 GPS、车载部分和主控中心等组成。其主要部件如图 6-4 所示。

主控中心

主控中心由电台、调制解调器、计算机系统和电子地图 4 部分组成。主控中心的电台用来接收汽车上电台发出的位置信息,同时也可反控汽车。调制解调器负责反控命令和 GPS 信息的数/模转换工作。计算机系统在接收到汽车的位置信息后,进行简单的预处理,然后按事先约定的通信协议,包装该信息并通过 RS 232 送往工作站。工作站则在矢量电子地图数据上显示汽车的位置,并提供空间查询功能。

车载部分

车载部分由 GPS 接收机、调制解调器及电台组成,有的还包括自律导航装置、车速传感器、陀螺传感器、CD-ROM 驱动器、LCD 显示器等。GPS 接收机用于接收 GPS 发射的信号。调制解调器用来控制 GPS 接收机的数据采集工作并将数据信息转换成模拟信号后再通过电台发往主控中心。

汽车电子导航系统工作原理

GPS 接收机接收 GFS 卫星信号,求出当前点的坐标、速度、时间等信息,当汽车行驶到地下隧道、高层楼群、高速公路或其他有遮掩物的地点而捕获不到 GPS 卫星信号时,系统可自动进入自律导航系统。

行车前,驾驶员把要去的城市、街道的名字用键盘输入计算机。计算机会借助卫星系统的信号导航,并根据车速传感器、方向传感器等实测的数据、目的地的方位,标明所去地点的最佳行车路线。驾驶员在行驶过程中可利用车内的显示装置,随时在屏幕上察看汽车所在地区的地图和汽车在地图上的精确位置。显示屏上还不断显示出到达目的地所剩的距离。

模块七　新能源汽车

文章 1　纯电动汽车的类型

纯电动汽车(简称 BEV),它是完全由可充电电池(如铅酸电池、镍镉电池、镍氢电池或锂离子电池)提供动力源的汽车。其主要组成如图 7-1 所示。

纯电动汽车有各种不同的分类方法,根据动力系统组件的多少和布置形式分类可分为以下几种。

常规(传统)型电动汽车

其动力传递路线见图7-2a)。这类电动汽车可直接由燃油汽车改装得到。其特点是仅用电动机和蓄电池系统取代传统的内燃机和燃油系统。由于其保留了传统内燃机汽车的变速器、主减速器和差速器等,因此对电动机的要求低,并可选择较小的电动机。

无变速器型电动汽车

其动力传递路线见图7-2b)。这类电动汽车的特点是用电动机和蓄电池系统取代传统的内燃机和燃油系统,并去掉了传统的内燃机汽车的变速器,电动机直接连接到传动轴,通过电动机的控制实现变速功能,虽然减少了车的质量和传动损失,但电动机的尺寸大。

无差速器型电动汽车

其动力传递路线见图7-2c)。这类电动汽车的特点是用电动机直接连接到左右两个驱动半轴上,结构简单,减少整车质量和传动损失,通过电动机的控制实现左右轮的差速和驱动力的分配。

电动轮型电动汽车

这类电动汽车主要由定子、永久磁铁、编码器、电动机线圈、轴承、行星齿轮和制动毂组成,见图7-2d)。其特点是无动力传递装置,把驱动电动机直接连接到驱动轮上,是结构最简单的电动汽车,空间利用率最大,无传动损失,但对驱动电动机的控制精度等要求高,并要求左右轮的转速之差满足汽车行驶特别是转弯时的要求。

文章2　纯电动汽车的结构和工作原理

结构

如图7-3所示,纯电动汽车装备有蓄电池、电动机、电动机控制装置和能源管理系等,能量的补充方式为充电,可在充电站或停车场进行,充电站使用的充电器多为快速充电器。由于电动机被拖动时,即可发电,因此纯电动汽车一般都带有可回收减速和下坡时能量回收(再生)系统。

工作原理

如图7-4所示,纯电动汽车是由蓄电池的能量使电机驱动车辆前进,电动汽车的工作原理:蓄电池→电流→电力调节器→电动机→动力传递系统→驱动汽车行驶。其中,蓄电池提供电流,经过电力调节器调节后输出到电动机,然后由电动机提供转矩,经传动装置后驱动车轮实现车辆行驶。

再生制动

电动汽车的再生制动,就是利用电机的电气制动产生反向力矩使车辆减速或停车。对于感应电机来说,电气制动有反接制动、直流制动和再生制动等。其中,能实现将制动过程中能量回收的只有再生制动。其本质是电机转子的转动频率超过电机的电源频率,电机处于发电状态,将机械能转化为电能,通过逆变器的反向续流二极管给电池充电。

文章3　混合动力汽车的类型

混合动力电动汽车是同时配备电力驱动系统和辅助动力单元的电动汽车,其中辅助动力单元是技术成熟的汽油机或柴油机,其主要组成如图 7-5 所示。混合动力电动汽车主要优点是发动机在经济工况区工作,排放低、燃油消耗少;发动机不在全负荷和加速工况工作,噪声小;可以回收制动时的能量和利用已有的燃油设备。它是当代汽车工业为保护大气环境及利用资源采取的重大技术措施。

根据动力系统的配置不同,混合动力系统可分为串联式、并联式和混联式。

串联式混合动力系统

串联式混合动力系统的结构如图 7-6 所示。其工作原理是发动机带动发电机发电,产生的电能一部分用来给蓄电池充电,另一部分通过电机控制器输送给电动机,由电动机产生电磁力矩驱动汽车行驶。

并联式混合动力系统

并联式混合动力系统的结构如图 7-7 所示。并联式混合动力系统包括内燃机和电机两套驱动系统,内燃机和电机可以分别独立地驱动汽车,需要大功率时还可由内燃机和电机共同驱动汽车,弥补了串联式混合动力系统最大功率不足的缺陷。

混联式混合动力系统

混联式混合动力系统的结构如图 7-8 所示。其工作原理是发动机产生的功率一部分通过机械传动装置输送给驱动桥,另一部分则驱动发电机发电,发出的电能输送给电机或蓄电池。电动机产生的力矩也可通过动力复合装置传送给驱动桥。根据行驶工况灵活采取串联方式或并联方式工作。

目前的混联式结构一般以行星齿轮机构作为动力复合装置。例如,丰田公司的 Prius 就采用了这种结构,它的驱动系统被公认为具有目前最成功的结构。

根据电池—电机与内燃机的搭配比例不同,可分为微混合、轻混合、全混合和可外接电源充电混合动力系统。

文章4　混合动力汽车的工作过程

如图 7-9 所示,以 THS(丰田汽车的混动系统)为例说明混合动力汽车的起步或低负荷行驶、匀速行驶、加速行驶、停车或滑行、制动和减速时系统的工作过程。

起步与小负荷时

车辆起步、极低速运行或在下陡坡时,发动机将在低效率区域中工作,故此时控制系统将切断燃油,使发动机停止工作。这时可以根据发动机发生空转与否判断是否切断燃油,利用电动机向车辆提供输出动力。电动机驱动车辆的路径如图 7-10 路径 A 所示。

正常行驶时

在正常行驶时发动机的动力通过动力分配机构分为两条输出通路,一条通路直接驱动车轮(图 7-11 路径 B),另一条通路驱动发电机使之发电,并用所发电能驱动电动机 5,从而增加车轮的驱动力(图7-11路径C)。这两条动力输出路径的关系是由计算机进行控制,使之达到最高效率。

全负荷加速时

全负荷加速时,除了上述正常行驶工况中所需的动力外,还要从蓄电池中输出电流,增加车轮的驱动力。车辆的动力如图7-12路径A、B、C所示。

在减速与制动时

在减速与制动时,车轮驱动电动机。这时,电动机变成了发电机,利用减速或制动的能量进行再生发电,把回收的能量存储在蓄电池中,如图7-13所示。

蓄电池充电时

对蓄电池进行控制,使之保持一定的充电状态。所以,当蓄电池的充电量减少时,通过发动机驱动发电机进行充电,直到使之达到规定的充电状态,如图7-14路径D所示。

停车时

车辆停止时,发动机也自动停止。没有常规发动机那样的怠速状态,无有害物和CO_2排放,同时也节约了能源。当蓄电池没达到规定的充电状态时,即使停车,发动机也会驱动发电机,通过路径D给蓄电池充电。当接通点火电源,汽车尚未起步时,发动机达到规定的温度状态后会自动停止运转。如果和空调开关联动的话,停车后发动机也会运转。

模块八　智能网联汽车

文章1　车载网络的主要类型

汽车技术领域的电子技术正在飞速发展。汽车电器日趋复杂、高度集成,使汽车工程师们必须寻求更快速有效的信息传输方式。总线技术在车辆上的应用,使汽车上更多更强的功能成为现实,如图8-1所示为总线技术在汽车上的应用。目前主要的总线类型如图8-2所示。

CAN 总线

CAN 是 Controller Area Network 的缩写。CAN 是 ISO 国际标准化的串行通信协议。在汽车产业中,出于对安全性、舒适性、方便性、低公害、低成本的要求,各种各样的电子控制系统被开发了出来,由于这些系统之间通信所用的数据类型及对可靠性的要求不尽相同,由多条总线构成的情况很多,线束的数量也随之增加。为了减少线束的数量以及进行大量数据的高速通信的需要,1986年德国电气商博世公司开发出面向汽车的 CAN 通信协议。此后,CAN 通过 ISO 11898 及 ISO 11519 进行了标准化,成为全球性的汽车网络的标准协议。

LIN 总线

LIN 总线是针对汽车分布式电子系统而定义的一种低成本的串行通领信网络,是对控制器区域网络(CAN)等其他汽车多路网络的一种补充,适用于对网络的带宽、性能或容错功能没有过高要求的应用。

MOST 总线

MOST 总线是宝马公司、戴姆勒克莱斯勒(DaimlerChrysler)公司、Harman/Becker 公司(音响系统制造商)和 Oasis Silicon Systems 公司联合开发的。MOST 总线专门用于满足要求严格的车载环境,这种新的基于光纤的网络能够支持 24.8Mbps 的数据速率,与以前的铜缆相比具有减轻重量和减小电磁干扰(EMI)的优势。

FlexRay 总线

FlexRay 是一种用于汽车的高速、可确定性的、具备故障容错能力的总线技术,它将事件触发和时间触发两种方式相结合,具有高效的网络利用率和系统灵活性特点,可以作为新一代汽车内部网络的主干网络。

蓝牙

蓝牙(Bluetooth)是无线网络传输技术的一种,原本是用来取代红外技术的。与红外技术相比,蓝牙无须对准就能传输数据,传输距离在 0~20 米(红外的传输距离在几米以内)。而在信号放大器的帮助下,通信距离甚至可达 100 米左右。而且,蓝牙设备之间还能传送声音、图像、视频等,如蓝牙耳机。

文章 2　CAN 网络

CAN 是 Controller Area Network 的缩写(以下称为 CAN),是 ISO 国际标准化的串行通信协议。CAN 总线的组成包括:数据总线、终端电阻、收发器、控制器、节点、网关等,见图 8-3。

数据总线

数据总线是控制单元间传递数字信号的通道,即所谓的信息高速公路。车载网络中的数据总线,类似于计算机网络中的网线。数据总线可以实现在一组数据线上传递的信号能同时被多个控制单元共享,从而最大限度地提高系统整体效率,充分利用有限的资源,见图 8-4。

CAN 总线分为 CAN 高位数据线(CAN-H)和 CAN 低位数据线(CAN-L),车上使用的大多数是双绞线的有线网络。

数据传输终端

终端电阻是网络的数据传输终端,通常是一个 120 Ω 的吸收电阻。它被用于阻止数据在传输终了被反射回来并产生反射波,因为反射波会破坏数据,见图 8-5。

CAN 收发器

收发器是一个发送器和接收器的组合。发送器的作用是将 CAN 控制器提供的数据转化为电信号并通过数据线发送出去;接收器的作用是接收总线上的数据,并将数据传送到 CAN 控制器。

CAN 控制器

控制器在 CPU 和 CAN 收发器之间接收、处理、传递数据。它接收 CPU 送来的数据、处理并传送给 CAN 收发器。同时,它接收 CAN 收发器传来的数据,处理并传送给 CPU。

节点

当我们使用计算机上网,通过某个网络平台与异地的另一台计算机通信,则两端的计算机就是网络中的两个节点,服务器终端也是一个节点。在车载网络中,节点即为与数据总线连接的控制单元见图8-6。

网关

网关的主要任务是使两个速度不同的系统之间能进行信息交换。网关相当于我们生活当中的火车站(图8-7)。在站台("站台"的英语也可译为"网关")A到达一列快车(CAN驱动数据总线,500kBit/s),车上有数百名旅客。在站台B已经有一辆火车(CAN舒适/Infotainment数据总线,100kBit/s)在等待,有一些乘客就换到这辆火车上,有一些乘客要换乘快车继续旅行。车站的这种功能,即让旅客换车,以便通过速度不同的交通工具到达各自目的地的功能,与CAN驱动数据总线和CAN舒适/Infotainment数据总线两系统网络的网关功能是相同的。

CAN总线的数据传递过程

(1)提供数据:节点中的CPU向CAN控制器发送数据,CAN控制器向CAN收发器提供需要发送的数据见图8-8。

(2)发送数据:所有节点都准备将数据向网络广播,优先权最高的节点的数据被发送。

(3)接收数据:所有其他节点转为接收器,都能接收到数据。

(4)检查数据:接收数据的节点检查、判断所接收的数据是否为本节点所需要的数据。

(5)接收数据:如数据对某节点重要,它将被该节点接收并进行处理,否则将被忽略。

文章3 智能网联汽车的概述

所谓"智能车辆",就是在普通车辆的基础上增加了先进的传感器(雷达、摄像)、控制器、执行器等装置(图8-9),通过车载传感系统和信息终端实现与人、车、路等的智能信息交换,使车辆具备智能的环境感知能力,能够自动分析车辆行驶的安全及危险状态,并使车辆按照人的意愿到达目的地,最终实现替代人来操作的目的。

从发展的角度,智能汽车将经历两个阶段。第一阶段是智能汽车的初级阶段,即辅助驾驶;第二阶段是智能汽车发展的终极阶段,即完全替代人的无人驾驶。美国高速公路安全管理局将智能汽车定义为以下5个层次:

(1)无智能化(层次0):由驾驶员每时每刻完全地控制汽车的原始底层结构,包括制动器、转向器、加速踏板以及起动机。

(2)具有特殊功能的智能化(层次1):该层次汽车具有一个或多个特殊自动控制功能,通过警告防范车祸于未然,可称之为"辅助驾驶阶段"。这一阶段的许多技术大家并不陌生,比如车道偏离警告系统(LDW)、正面碰撞警告系统(FCW)、盲点信息(BLIS)系统。

(3)具有多项功能的智能化(层次2):该层次汽车具有至少融合实现两个原始控制功能的系统,完全不需要驾驶员对这些功能进行控制,可称之为"半自动驾驶阶段"。这个阶段的汽车会智能地判断司机是否对警告的危险状况作出响应,如果没有,则替司机采取行动,比如紧急自动制动系统(EAB)、紧急车道辅助系统(ELA)。

(4)具有限制条件的无人驾驶(层次3):该层次汽车能够在某些特定的驾驶环境下让驾驶员完全不用控制汽车,而且汽车可以自动检测环境的变化以判断是否转为驾驶员驾驶模式,可称之为"高度自动驾驶阶段"。谷歌无人驾驶汽车基本处于这个层次。

(5)全工况无人驾驶(层次4):该层次汽车完全自动控制车辆,全程检测交通环境,能够实现所有的驾驶目标,驾驶员只需要提供目的地或者输入导航信息,在任何时候都不需要对车辆进行操控,可称之为"完全自动驾驶阶段"或者"无人驾驶阶段"。

文章4　智能网联汽车关键技术

智能网联汽车是指搭载先进传感器、控制器、执行器等装置(图8-10),融合现代通信与网络技术,实现车与X(人、车、路、后台等)的智能信息交换共享,具备复杂的环境感知、智能决策、协同控制和执行等功能的新一代汽车。近年来,随着汽车产业的发展,并逐步向着"自动化、智能化、网络化、共享化"转型。谷歌、微软、百度等互联网巨头,以及特斯拉等高科技企业纷纷入局。智能网联汽车进入高速发展阶段,成为时下最火热的技术。

环境感知技术

环境感知系统的任务是利用摄像头、雷达、超声波等主要车载传感器以及V2X通信系统感知周围环境,通过提取路况信息、检测障碍物,为智能网联汽车提供决策依据(图8-11)。由于车辆行驶环境复杂,当前感知技术在检测与识别精度方面无法满足自动驾驶发展需要。深度学习被证明在复杂环境感知方面有巨大优势。在传感器领域,目前涌现了不同车载传感器融合的方案,用以获取丰富的周边环境信息。高精度地图与定位也是车辆重要的环境信息来源。

自主决策技术

决策机制应在保证安全的前提下适应尽可能多的工况,进行舒适、节能、高效的正确决策。常用的决策方法有状态机、决策树、深度学习、增强学习等。状态机用有向图表示决策机制,具有高可读性,能清楚表达状态间的逻辑关系,但需要人工设计,不易保证状态复杂时的性能。决策树是一种广泛使用的分类器,具有可读的结构。它可以通过样本数据的训练来建立,但是有过拟合的倾向,需要广泛的数据训练。它的效果与状态机类似,可以应用于部分工况的自动驾驶。深度学习与增强学习在处理自动驾驶决策方面,能通过大量的学习实现在复杂工况下的决策,并能进行在线的学习优化,但在未知工况下的性能不易明确。

控制执行技术

控制系统的任务是控制车辆的速度与行驶方向,使其跟踪规划的速度曲线与路径。现有自动驾驶技术多数针对常规工况,较多采用传统的控制方法。它的性能可靠、计算效率高,已在主动安全系统中得到应用。现有控制器的工况适应性是一个难点,可根据工况参数进行控制器参数的适应性设计。在控制领域中,多智能体系统是由多个具有独立自主能力的智能体通过一定的信息拓扑结构相互作用而形成的一种动态系统。用多智能体系统方法来研究车辆队列,可以显著降低油耗、改善交通效率以及提高行车安全性。

通信与平台技术

车载通信的模式,依据通信的覆盖范围可分为车内通信、车际通信和广域通信。车内通信,从蓝牙技术发展到 Wi-Fi 技术和以太网通信技术;车际通信,包括专用的短程通信技术和正在建立标准的车间通信长期演进技术;广域通信,指目前广泛应用在移动互联网领域的 5G 等通信方式。通过网联无线通信技术,车载通信系统将更有效地获得的驾驶员信息、自车的姿态信息和汽车周边的环境数据,并进行整合与分析。车辆通过车与云平台的通信将其位置信息及运动信息发送至云端,云端控制器结合道路信息以及交通信息对车辆速度和挡位等进行优化,以提高车辆燃油经济性并提高交通效率。

信息安全技术

结合智能网联汽车发展实际,确定网联数据管理对象并实行分级管理,建立数据存储安全、传输安全、应用安全 3 个维度的数据安全体系。建立包括云安全、管安全、端安全在内的数据安全技术框架,制定智能网联数据安全技术标准。围绕信息安全技术领域的周边行业,出现很多创新研究方向。比如在信息安全测试评估方面,通过干扰车辆的通信设备以及雷达和摄像头等车载传感设备,进行智能车的信息安全的攻防研究。

附件2 汽车专业词汇(检索 A-Z)

A

A/C clutch	空调离合器
A/C compressors	空调压缩机
A/C outlets	空调出口
A/C pressure transducer	空调压力传送器
A/C request	空调需求指示器
A/C system module	空调系统模块
ABS	防抱死制动系统
AC-DC converter	交/直流转换器
AC-DC inverter	交/直流倒相器
acceleration shock testers	加速冲击测试机
accelerator pedal	加速踏板
access to the fiber optics controller area network(CAN)	区域网(CAN)光纤控制器插入口
accumulator/dehydrator	储液/干燥器
acoustic performance	流体动力学性能
active crossovers	有源分频放大器
active matric liquid crystal display(AMLCD)	有源矩阵液晶显示
active roll control system	主动式侧倾控制系统
actuator	执行器
adaptive cruise control	车速控制自动调整
adaptive restraint technologies	自动调整式乘员保护技术
adaptive ride suspensions	自动调节式行驶悬架
adaptive seating system	自动调节式座椅
AdCat	吸附式催化转换器
add-on	售车后加装产品
adjustable outside handle lever clip	可调式车外手柄夹杆
adjuster	调节器
advanced propulsion system	先进的推进系统
advanced ride control suspension system	先进行驶控制悬架系统
advantage of long range	长程行驶优势

aftermarket	售后市场
aiming requirement	聚光照明要求
air cleaner	空气滤清器
air ducts	风道
air meter	气流计,风速表
air/fuel management	空气和燃油供给管理系统
air/fuel subsystem	空气和燃油供给子系统
air/fuel system	空气/燃料系统
airbag	安全气囊
airbag cushion	安全气囊垫
airbag door	安全气囊门盖
airbag inflation simulation	安全气囊充气模拟分析
airborne particle analysis	空中尘粒分析
airlift	气举式
airlift assists	气举式辅助功能
algorithms and software	算法语言规则系统及软件
alignment features	准直定位装置
all-belts-to-seat	安全带及座椅一体化系统
alternate hide coverings	备用替代蒙皮
Alternating or sequential injection	交替或顺序喷射
alternators	交流发电机
aluminum die cast and steel hybrid	铝压铸与钢复合
AM/FM-AM/FM	频道(调幅/调频)
anechoic sound chamber	吸音室,隔音室
angle capacity	角度转动能力
antenna	天线
anti-lock brake system	防抱死制动系统
anti-theft switches	防盗开关
anticipatory control	提前控制
anticipating crash sensing	撞击提前感测
aqueous washes and vacuum-degreasers	水洗和真空除油工艺
assembly labor	装配劳力
assembly modules	组装模件
assembly tooling	装配工具
attached rods	连接杆
automated assembly station	自动化装配站
automated part identification	部件自动识别
automated pull-to-seat	自动牵入定位

automatic highway system (AHS)	自动化高速公路系统
axle stroking force	轴向冲程力
axle boot covers	车轴防尘罩

B

back shrouds	后护板
back-up aid system	倒车辅助系统
back pressure EGR	背压废气再循环
bag dynamics/kinematics	安全气囊动态/运动特性
ball groove	球道
base plate	基板
basic composite upper intake manifolds	复合顶部进油口歧管
bass by-noise legislation	移动噪声限制规范
battery backup sounder	后备电池警笛
battery module	蓄电池模块
battery operating range	蓄电池支持形成能力
BEC	母线电气中心
Bill-of-Materials data	原料单数据
blade	插片
body electronics computer	车身电子计算机
body electronics	车身电子装置
bolt-together	螺接(拴接)
Booster-Single, Tandem, Tie rod	助力器-单件式, 串联式, 细杆式
boot sealing system	轴套密封系统
box design	盒形设计
brake apply component	制动执行部件
brake balance	均衡制动功能
brake booster mounting	制动助理器固定架
brake corner modules	制动组件(模块)
brake proportioner	"制动比例"调节器
brake-by-wire technology	电线制动技术
brake-by-wire	电线制动
brush life	碳刷寿命
build process	开发过程
building block	积木式
built-in flame arrestor	内置消焰器
built-in hydrometer	内置液体比重计
bulkhead	隔板连接
bump technology	缓撞技术

bussed electrical center	母线电气中心
bussing configuration	母线配置

C

cable core	电缆芯
CAD "soft gauge"	CAD"软测规"
caliper	铝质制动钳
calorimeter	热量计
cam phaser & solenoid	凸轮相位器电磁线圈
cam phasing	可变凸轮相位器
camshaft, crankshaft and combustion sensors	凸轮轴、曲轴和燃烧传感器
canister purge	油气收集碳罐清洗脱附
cap lock	盖罩锁定
cardan joint	万向节
cast skin	表层铸造
catalyst coating module	触媒涂覆模块
catalyst light-off solutions	催化剂起燃溶液
catalytic converters	催化转换器
cavities	插线孔
cavity plugs	堵头
cell connector	电池接头
cell phone	车载电话
cellular phone	车载电话
center console switch package	中央仪表盘开关组
center high mounted stop lamps	中间高位制动灯
centered plate strap	分中布置的板极条
central locking	中央锁定,中央锁定装置
challenge and response crypt code	双向时变密码
charge air cooler	充气冷却器,中冷器
chassis corner modules	底盘拐弯模块
check call outs for validity	检查提取数据的有效性
child safety mechanism	儿童安全保护机构
circuit density	电路密度
climate control system	汽车空调系统
climate control	汽车空调
climate wind tunnels	气候风洞
clip	线夹
close-coupled	紧凑耦合安装式
closed-loop air/fuel ration feedback	闭环控制系统空气/燃料混合比反馈信息

closed-loop process-controlled injection mold machine	闭路过程控制注塑成型机
clutch cycling	周期性离合动作
clutch linkage	离合器连杆机构
cockpit module	驾驶舱模块
coil over shock absorber	套在减振器外的螺旋弹簧
coil per cylinder	一个缸配一个点火线圈
cold formed outer ball groove	冷成型外球槽
cold rolled-expanded lead calcium grid	冷碾压铅钙极板
cold formed	冷成型
collapse load, distance and dynamics	破坏负荷、压缩距离和动态参数
collapse load	破坏负荷
collar	轴承环
collision avoidance processor	防撞车微处理机
collision intervention processor	防撞干预处理器
collision warning system	防撞预警系统
column covers	转向盘柱盖板
combustible mixture of fuel and air	可燃混合气
comfortable ride	舒适型驾驶
common corner concept	公用拐弯件概念
communication link	通信线路
communication system	通信系统
compact disc / compact disc changer	光盘机/多光盘换放机
compact variable compressor	小型可变排气压缩机
compartment latching system	车厢锁扣系统
compatible terminals	兼容端子
complete wheel-to-wheel modules	完整的车轮到车轮模块
composite headlight modules	复合前照灯模块
composite structural bead	复合结构梁
composite upper intake manifolds	复合式进气歧管
compression sense	压缩传感器
Computational Fluid Dynamics	(CFD)计算流体动力学分析方法
computer simulation and modeling	计算机模拟和原型设计
computer-aided design	(CAD)计算机辅助设计
computing and networking standards	电脑化和网络化标准装置
concentric isolator	同心隔离装置
connector index change	接头标号
connector position assurance	(CPA)连接定位组件;连接器定位组件

connector seal	连接器密封
console or lower extension	仪表板或下面扩展部分
constant velocity joints	等速万向节
continuous variable real-time damping system	连续变化实时减震系统
continuously variable joint(CV)	连续变速(CV)万向节
controlled suspension system	受控悬架系统
converging technology	集合技术
cool-to-the-touch	触手不烫
core	暖风芯子,核心
core sizes	芯体规格
core wings	芯管
corner brake module	制动组件
corner module (low mass)	轻型底盘模块
cornering lamp	转向指示灯
corona	电晕
cost efficiency	成本效益比,性能价格比
courtesy	门控灯
courtesy lamp switches	门控灯开关
cover materials	外层材料
cover retainer	外壳固定件
cover with splice tape	带分接胶带的盖板
crank wheel	曲柄轮
cranking inhibitor	熄火防止器
crankshaft sensor	曲轮传感器
crash severity sensing	撞击严重程度监测
crashworthiness	减少车祸伤害
Creative Solutions	创造性解决方案
crimp strength	压接强度
crimped splice	有折皱的线路连接方式
crimpless conductive path	无折皱导电通道
cross sectional views	剖视图
cross-car beam integration	横梁整合技术
cross-flow	水平流式
cross-groove joint	叉槽式万向节
cruise control system	巡航车速控制系统
crypt code	时变密码
cup holders	饮料杯固定架
current capability	载流量

current rating	额定电流值
customer benefits	用户利益
customer center	客户中心(大楼)
customer director	(客户服务)专职经理
Customer Focused	以客为尊,以客户为重点
customer support engineer	(CSE)客户支持工程师(统一管理计划)
cut leads	切割线头
CVC	紧凑可变排量压缩机
CVRTD damper	连续变化实时减振器
cycle life	使用寿命

D

damper modules	减振器模块
damper by-wire	电子伺服悬架控制
damper	减振器,缓冲装置
data channels	计算机数据通道
daytime running lamps (DRL)	白天驾驶灯
deactivation	功能关闭装置
dead bolt locking	锁柱锁定装置
deck lid latch	行李舱盖锁扣
defogger	除雾器
delayed interior lamp	车内灯延迟关闭功能
Delphi	德尔福汽车系统
Delphi Delco	德尔福德科电子系统分部
Delphi's E-Loc System	德尔福 E-Loc 系统
demonstration vehicle	示范样车
deployment openings	打开位置
depowering	能量降低装置
designed-in sound	预置音响系统
detent sensing switches	锁销传感开关
diagnostic solenoids	诊断电磁线圈
diagnostic connector	诊断接头
diagnostic interfaces	诊断接口
diagnostic probe	诊断探头
DIC	驾驶员信息中心组合开关
die-cast Mg insert	铸镁嵌埋件
die-cast magnesium steering wheel insert	模铸镁质转向盘插入件
digital audio broadcast	数字式广播频道
digital playback	数字式放音机

digital signal processing	数字信号处理
digital versatile disc	数字式通用光盘机
digital voice amplifier	数字式音频放大器
dimmer switch	灯光调暗开关
diode pack	二极管组件
dip	浸胶
direct acting outside handle	直拉式车外手柄
dis-(arming) alarm system	触发警报系统
disc & drum corner assemblies	盘式和鼓式制动组件
discrete packages	离散照明封装件
dissipater	消散装置
dissipaters (calorimeters)	热交换器风洞(热量计)
distribute drawings	分发图样(配电图)
distributed / non-distributed	分布／非分布式
distributed electronic products	分配电子产品
distributed lighting high intensity discharge lamps	分布式照明高强投射灯
distributor-based	分配器为基础的(点火系统)
disturbance	扰动
dive	前倾
diversity	分集天线
diversity antenna	分集天线系统
dock and lock cluster	对接锁定集束
dome light switch	车顶灯开关
door ajar switch	车门微启开关
door ajar switches	半开门开关
door deployment	车门配置
door handle lights	车门把手灯
door hardware module	车门锁件模块
door hardware system	车门锁件系统
door latch	车门锁扣
door modules and related hardware	车门模件及相关硬件
door trim	车门饰件
double offset joint	标准梅花形接头
down-flow	垂直流式
drive-by-wire technology	靠电线驾驶技术
drive-by-wire	靠电线驾驶
driveline lash	传动系游隙
driveline system	传动系(统)

driver warning signal	向驾驶员提供预警信号
drum	制动鼓
drum brake assembly	鼓式制动器组件
dual internal fan construction	内置双风扇
dual sided seat recliner	双扶手座椅倾斜调节器
dual tank	并列集流室
dual-lock tangs	双重锁定作用的凸舌
dual-stage crimping	两极压接
duct work	布线管
duo servo	双紧蹄制动器
dust shields	防尘罩
dynamic rear proportioning variable effort steering	动态后部比例齿轮齿调(条)式转向机
dynamics	动态安全数据
dynamometer testing	测功试验,测力试验

E

ECM	发动机控制模块
EGR	废气再循环
EPS	电动转向系统
elastomer dome soft-touch switch	弹性橡胶软触开关
elastomer dome switch	弹性橡胶开关
electric or hydraulic rear wheel brakes	后轮电动或液压制动器
electric power steering	电(气)动(力)转向
electrical architecture	电路结构
electrical centers	电路中心
electrical/electronic connection systems	电气/电子结配系统
electro-hydraulic power steering	电动-液压动力转向
electro-motor cruise control	电机控制的稳速装置
electronic CAD link-ups	CAD 计算机联机
electronic control heads	电子控制板
electronic control module	电子控制模块(ECMs)
electronic control modules and algorithms	电子控制模块与规则系统
electronic headers	电子集束连接装置
electronic throttle control	节气阀电子控制装置
electronic variable orifice	电子可调节气孔
electronically enhanced vehicle systems	电子加强汽车系统技术装备
electronic control heads	电子控制头
elliptical beam system	椭圆光束系统
EMI	电磁干扰

EMS	发动机管理系统
enclosed stator	封闭式定子
encrypted rolling code	预编滚动代码
endgate latch	后舱门锁扣
energy absorbing column	可调式吸能转向管柱
energy management package	能源管理成套系统
energy storage and conversion	能源储存和转换系统
engage force	咬合力
engine compartment fluids	发动机腔室流体
engine cooling fan	发动机冷却风扇
engine dynamometer	发动机台架试验
entry/ignition system	插入/点火系统
environmental aging	受环境影响的老化
equalizer	均衡器
ergonomics	人机功效(学)
EVAP canister	油气收集碳罐(燃油蒸发物收集碳罐)
evaporative emissions canisters	油气收集碳罐
exhaust aftertreatment	排气后处理系统
exhaust gas recirculation valves	排气再循环阀
exhaust gas recirculation	废气再循环
exhaust systems	排气系统
external component design	外部零件设计
external lock	外锁定件

F

failure Mode Analysis	故障形态分析
fiber optic connectors	光纤连接器
filler neck	注油口
Finite Element Analysis	有限元分析
Finite Element Modeling	有限元模型设计
fire stroke	燃油冲程
fixed displacement	固定排量
fixture	夹具
flat panel	平面显示屏
flat panel display	平面仪表板显示器
flat plate design	平板式设计
flat plate oxygen	平板氧传感器
flat response knock sensor	平态响应爆震传感器
flex-pin	弯脚针

flexible circuits	活动电路
flexible coupling	挠性联轴节
flexible printed circuit	挠性印刷电路
foam injection process	薄膜喷注工艺
follow the customer	跟随客户走(策略)
footwell light	踏脚灯
forewarn	防撞预警系统
forward lighting systems	前视照明系统
forward looking system	前视系统
forward millimeter wave radar	厘米波长前视雷达
foundation brake	主制动器
four wheel steering	四轮转向
free space	自由空间
free wheeling handle levers	转动手柄可自由移动
free wheeling key cylinder lever	插匙锁心杆可自由旋转
free-motion joint	自由运动万向节
front-steer-by-wire	电子伺服前轮转向控制
front/rear seat	前后座椅控制
front detection sensor	前方监测传感器
front end module	前端模块
front oxygen sensor	前氧传感器
front airbag modules and control electronics	前侧安全气囊模块及控制电子装置
front light	前照灯
fuel cells	燃料电池组
fuel economy	节油效率
fuel efficiency	燃油效率
fuel efficiency and performance system	节油及性能系统
fuel efficient chassis	高油效底盘
fuel handling and evaporative emissions systems	燃油供给与蒸气回收控制系统
fuel handling and evaporative	燃油输送和蒸发排放控制系统
fuel injected four cylinder engines	燃油喷射四缸发动机
fuel injection	燃油喷射
fuel injectors	燃油喷嘴
fuel pressure regulator	燃油压力调节器
fuel pump and sender assemblies	燃油泵和油位传感器总成
fuel pump relay	输油泵继电器
fuel rail	燃油导轨
fuel tank energy storage	油箱蓄能器

full car control	整车控制
full magnesium die casting	全镁压铸
full service vehicle wiring systems	汽车全套布线系统
fully anechoic sound chamber	全吸音声学实验室
fully integrated 3-dimensional CAD CAM system	整体合成三维 CAD/CAM 系统
functional temp. range	适用温度范围

G

gauging	测量定规
gear level indicator switch	自动变速挡位指示开关
Gen. Ⅱ HTC	第二代平行流式
Gen. Ⅲ bearings	第三代轴承
Gen. Ⅲ wheel bearings	第三代车轮轴承
general power splicing	一般动力连接
Generation Ⅲ hydraulic element assembly	第三代液压元件组件
generous electrolyte reservoir	大容积电解液槽
glare	眩光
glass breakage sensor	车窗破裂传感器
glass drive switch	车窗玻璃升降开关
global customer support network	全球客户支持网
Global Partnerships	全球伙伴关系
global positioning system	全球定位系统
global positioning system / cellular	全球定位系统/车载电话天线
Globalization	全球化
glove box assembly	小工具组件
gold-plated cross-point technology	镀金交叉点技术
good EMC performance	电磁相容性好
GPS	全球定位系统
GQS (global quality system)	全球质量系统
grid corrosion	铅板腐蚀
ground clearance	离地高度
ground illumination	底面照明灯(泥水灯)
grounded	搭铁
GT Connection System	GT 连接装置
guard	护板

H

halfshaft assemblies	半轴组件
halfshaft assembly	半轴总成
Hall crank position sensor	霍尔效应曲柄位置传感器

halogen infrared (HIR)	卤素红外光灯
hand tooling	手动工具
handling maneuvers	操纵行为
hands-free power opening and closing	"不用手"电动开门和关门机构
hardboard circuits	硬板电路
harness manufacturer	电路线束生产厂
harness strain relief	线束固定张力释放
harness-integrated electrical center	由电路集束组成的电气中心
harness-integrated modules	含有电路线束的模块
harness-to-harness interconnects	线束间直接连接
hazard warning flasher switch	低电源危险预警闪光指示灯开关
head restraint	头部保护装置
head-up display	平视显示器
header	集束连接装置
headered tube and center design	盖管核心型
headered tube and centered design	平行流式
heat sealed cover	热封盖
heat treating	热处理
heat/shield inflator retainer	阻热充气装置挡板
heater cores	暖风芯子
heating the passenger compartment	驾驶室(乘客仓)采暖
heating, ventilation and air conditioning modules	冷暖风空调系统模块
heave	上跳
height sensor	高度传感器
high current	高电流
high intensity discharge (HID)	高强度氙气灯
high performance	性能优异
High Performance Test Management	高性能测试管理系统
high retention seat	记忆型座椅
high-performance interconnects	高性能互连装置
high-speed film coverage	高速电影摄像记录
highway loads	高速公路负荷指标
hinged cover	铰接盖罩
hold-down configuration	适合下插式安装
holder	座架
hot, ambient, cold preconditions	高温、常温和低温条件预设
housing base	容器底座
human machine interface	人机对话接口

Hybrid Ⅲ dummies Hybrid	Ⅲ型人体模型
Hybrid Ⅲ torso with instrumentation	配有测试仪器的 Hybrid Ⅲ型人体模型
hybrid rotor	混合型转子
hydraulic front wheel brakes	前轮液压制动器
hydraulic solenoid coil	液压电磁线圈
hydraulic solenoid switch	液压电磁开关
hydraulic variable orifice	液压可调节气孔径
hydrocarbon absorber	碳氢化合物吸收装置
hydrostatic force and deceleration sled test	液体静力和减速橇测试
hytrel	油封

I

idle air control	怠速空气控制
idle speed	怠速
ignition cable system	点火线系统
ignition cables and assemblies	点火线和组件
ignition coil and electronics	点火线圈和电子元件
ignition coils and drivers	点火线圈和驱动器
ignition modules	点火模块
ignition systems	点火系统
ignition wiring products	点火线路产品
ignition starter switch	点火起动器开关
illuminated entry	车门入口照明
illuminated entry switches	车门入口照明开关
immobilization	密码转发器防盗
immobilizer	密码转发器防盗锁
immobilize	使汽车无法起动
in-line connections	在线连接装置
in-line electric drive unit	已经连线的电气驱动装置
in-lines	在线连接件
in-mold painting	型内喷漆
in-molding technology	同时模压涂层技术
in-tank applications	装于散热器水箱内
in-tank transmission and engine oil cooler	箱内埋置式变速器及发电机油冷器
inclination sensing	倾斜传感装置
inclination sensor	倾斜传感器
induction temperature sensor	感应空气温度传感器
inductive coupled SIR/Pad control	电感耦合 SIR/减震垫控制器
inflator	充气装置

inflator ballistics testing	充气装置冲击测试
inflators	(安全气囊)气体发生器
injection fuel filters	喷射燃油滤清器
injection mold	注射模型
injection molding	注射模压技术
injection-molding facility	注射成型设备
inlet air temperature	进气温度
inner connector	内部连接器
inner panel	内护板
innovation	技术革新
insert (steering wheel insert)	骨架
inserts	镶套
inside door handle	车门内手柄
inside handle override	车内手柄超越控制
instrument panel	仪表盘
Insulation Displacement Connections (IDC)	绝缘位移连接技术
intake air flow	进入发动机的空气流量
intake oil flow	油入口流量
integral multi-function IC regulator	多功能集成电路调节器
integral steering gears	整体式转向机(循环球式转向机)
integral steering wheel and driver airbag module	转向盘和驾驶侧安全气囊整合式模块
integrated air fuel module	一体化空气/燃油模块
integrated body	集成车身
integrated cockpit module	集成式驾驶舱模块
integrated electronic cartridge	整合电子模块
integrated electro-hydrolic apply modulator and controller	一体化的电动-液压执行元件和控制器
integrated electronic cartridge	集成电子插块
integrated electronics controls	电子集成控制件
integrated flex circuits	集成挠性线路
integrated intelligent chassis control system	智能底盘控制一体化系统
integrated power lock actuator	整合式电动锁起动装置
intelligent highway	智能高速公路
intelligent audio amplifier	智能音频放大器
intelligent brake control system	智能制动控制系统
integral gear	整体式转向机
Interior & Lighting Systems	内饰及照明系统
interior dome lights	车顶灯

interior lamp dimming	车内灯调节功能
interior trim deformation	车内装饰板的变形
intermediate drive shaft	中间驱动轴
intermediate shaft	中间轴
intermediate steering shafts	中间转向轴
Intermodel Surface Transportation Efficiency Act (ISTEA)	陆地联运效率法
internal combustion engine primary power	内燃发动机一次电源
internet access	网络接入口
ion sense ignition	离子传感点火技术
IP cluster	组合仪表板灯
IR transreceiver (multimedia personal computer)	红外发收器(多媒体个人电脑)

J

jacketed automotive cables	汽车用线束
jamb switch	门窗侧壁开关
JIT (just in time delivery)	"无仓库供货"
joint	万向节
joint type	接头类型
jounce bumpers	弹簧减振器
junction blocks	连接块
just-in-time delivery	无仓库供货

K

key buzzer switch	钥匙蜂鸣开关
key only locking	只用钥匙锁定
knee bolster	膝枕
knee restraints	膝盖保护装置
knock sensor	爆震传感器
knock	爆震
knuckle	(铝质)转向节

L

lane tracking	车行路线选择
lap-lock	搭接锁定
lash adjuster	间隙调节器
latching systems	车锁系统
lateral accelerometer yaw rate sensor	横向加速度计侧滑速率感受器
lead time	开发生产准备周期
leaded fuel	含铅燃油
leading trailing	前导牵引

lean	精简
Lean Manufacturing	精益生产
leather-wrapped	外包皮革
leg room	伸腿空间
lens optics	前照灯闪光玻璃罩
light control module (LCM)	照明控制模块
light output mechanism	光亮输出端
light-off	关灯
lightweight brake corner modules	轻质制动模块
lightweight rotor	轻质制动盘
liquid/gas separator	液/器分离器
LITEFLEX＊＊R composite leaf springs	LITEFLEX＊＊R复合材料叶片弹簧
load cell crimp inspection	压接检验
load control multiplexing	多路传输负荷控制
lock cartridge module	锁头模块(件)
lock rod	锁栓
low energy resistance	低能电阻
low pressure gas charging	低压充气
low profile	结构扁平
low-end torque	下限转矩
low-energy circuits	低能耗电路
low-mass design	轻质设计
low-mount passenger airbag	低位乘员安全气囊
low-profile switch	扁平开关
lower shroud	下护板
lower control arm	铝质低位控制臂
lumbar support	腰部支撑
Lumped Resistance	集中电阻

M

machining	机加工
magmeter sensor	测速器传感器
magnetic noise	磁噪
magnetic variable assistant steering	磁力可变辅助转向
magneto resistive	抗磁阻
male blade	阳插片
male cap assembly	阳盖插头组件
male pin	阳插脚
malfunction indicator light	故障指示灯

manifold converters	排气歧管转换器
manual child security levers	保护儿童安全手动杆
manual fore/aft, lift seat adjuster (hybrid)	座椅前/后及抬升手动调节器(混合型)
manual seat adjuster with modular tracks	带模块式轨道的手动座椅调节器
manual selectable ride system	人工可选行驶控制系统
map sensor	进气歧管绝对压力(微型)传感器
map system	地图系统
mapping system	地图定位技术
mass	物质量
mass flow	质量流量
master cylinder	制动总泵
master digital engine	数字式主机
math model	数理模型
max/min tolerance zones	最大/最小公差范围区
mechanical foam	机加工泡沫垫
mechanical shock	机械冲击
mechanical-assist	机械辅助
mechatronic-hydraulic steering system	机械电子-液压结合转向系统
membrane horn switch two-shot cover	汽车喇叭薄膜开关双色盖
membrane horn switch	汽车喇叭薄膜开关
memory mirror	带记忆功能的外后视镜
memory seat	带记忆功能的电动座椅
metal forming	金属成型
micro alloy coil springs	微合金螺旋弹簧
Micro-Pack in-lines Micro-Pack	在线连接件
mini disc / mini disc changer	微型光盘/微型多光盘换放机
Mini-Wedge **R latches	伟绩**R车门锁
misfire	缺火
mobile media	车载媒体
modeling expertise	模型分析专有技术
modem	调制解调器
modular aluminum shock absorbers	模块式铝质减振器
modular build technology	模块式开发技术
modular cockpit	模块式座舱
modular design	模块式设计
modular fuel pump & sender	燃油泵和输送器总成
modular fuel sender assemblies	整体式燃油供给系统总成
modular integration	模块式集成方法

modular strut	柱式减振器
modulator and controller	调节器和控制器
molded polarity	模块式极性符号
molded urethane	模塑聚氨酯产品
molded-in handling aids	模件造型内含装配辅助点
monoleaf composite spring	单叶式复合弹簧
monotube leveling	单管调平功能
monotube shock	单管减振器
motor/generator secondary power	电动机/发电机二次电源
movable reflector/fixed lens	移动式反光镜/固定反光罩
multec Ⅱ injector	马尔特克Ⅱ型喷油器
multi-antenna module	多元天线模块
multi-channel discreet equalization	多频道离散均衡器
multi-gauge system	多线规连接系统
multi-link rear suspension modules	多点连接后悬架模块
multi-port fuel injection throttle bodies	多喷口燃油喷射节流阀
multiple levels of inflation and automatic suppression	多级膨胀与自动压缩技术
multiple video displays	多路图像显示
multiplex systems	多功能通信系统

N

navigation	导航
noise measurement tools	噪声测量设备
noise suppression	噪声抑制
non-grounded	非搭铁
Non-linear F.E.A.	非线性 F.E.A.
nondestructive troubleshooting	非破坏性故障检修
nose piece	突鼻组件

O

OBD Ⅱ	第二代车载诊断系统
obstacle detection and avoidance	路障检测及避让
occupant accessory system (OAS)	乘员附件系统
occupant environment systems	乘员环境系统
occupant position and posture sensing	乘员位置及姿势感测
occupant proximity sensing	乘员防撞感测
occupant simulation	乘员模拟分析
occupant weight sensing	乘员体重感测
octane switch	辛烷开关

oil cooler	油冷器
oil economy	节油性能
on-glass	窗式天线
on-target fuel delivery	额定燃油输送率
one-piece silicone overmold	整体式硅酮面塑层
one-piece silicone switch pad	整体式硅胶开关垫
optic distributed lighting bundles	光纤分配照明线束
optical star coupler	光纤星形耦合器
optional anticipatory control	替代型预感(驾驶员意图)控制
Optional ZEV Mode	零尾气排放任选模式
optional	加装件
orifice tube (OT)	孔管(OT)系统
orifice tube	节流孔管
OT	毛细管系统
outer ball groove	外球道
overcharge	过充电
overhead console	车顶盒
oxygen sensors	氧气传感器

P

PACE (Premier automotive supplier's contribution to excellence)	优秀汽车供应商卓越奖计划奖
packaging	封装
padding	衬垫
painted and unpainted black	喷漆型和未喷漆型黑色
panel mount connection	仪表板安装接头
parallel hybrid vehicle	并联混合动力汽车
park brake switch	停(驻)车制动开关
part of door module assembly	车门模块组件部件
partial instrument panel pads (with a lower carrier)	部分仪表盘底盘(带下托架)
PASDS	动力和信号分配系统
pass key	加密钥匙
pass lock	加密锁
passive optical star coupler	无源光学星形耦合器
passive restraint switches	被动式限制开关
path tracking	道路附着力
PCB	印刷电路板
pedal feel	制动踏板力感

performance advantages	性能优势
peirmeter lighting functions	汽车周边照明
permietric alarm	车身周边警报功能
personal services	个人服务
phone booster	电话增音器
pilot build	样车建造
pitch conditions	倾斜调整
plastic molding	塑料模压
plastic optical fiber	塑性光纤
plate type oil cooler	板式油冷却器
plates made from high-density paste	高密度板极
platform	汽车底盘
POF data transmission	POF 数据传输
point-to-point connection system	点到点连接系统
poison resistance	防中毒性能
polypropylene case	聚丙烯壳体
port fuel injection and throttle body injection	多点式燃油喷射与节气阀体喷射系统
port fuel injection	多点式燃油喷射系统
position-control steering actuator	位置控制转向执行器
positive connector seal retention (PLR)	正向连接带密封保持
post-painted colors	后期喷漆色彩
pot-style joint	管筒型万向节
power actuator	电动执行机构
Power and Signal Distribution	动力与信号分配
power application	动力应用(场合)
power assist parallel hybrids	动力辅助并联混合系统
power brake module	助力制动模块
power circuit	动力电路
power closers	动力开门装置
power conversion electronics	动力转换电子装置
power deck lid	电动行李舱盖
power generation and storage systems	发电及动力储存系统
power hatch	电动行李舱盖锁
power in	电源接通
power lift gate	电动后仓门
power locking/unlocking	电动锁定/松释
power out	电源切断
power products	电动产品系统

power seat	动力座椅
power seat adjusters	动力座椅调节器
power sliding door	电动滑动车门
power sliding glass	电动滑窗
power steering pumps	动力转向泵
power sunroof controller	活动顶棚动力控制器
power-assist parallel hybrid propulsion	动力辅助并联混合推进系统
power chain cooling system	发动机变速器冷却系统
power train	动力总成
power train control module	动力总成控制模块(PCMs)
power train cooling system	发动机/变速器冷却系统
precision purge solenoid	精密净化电磁线圈
press-fit diode	压合连接式二极管
pressure feedback transducer	压力反馈传感器
pressure regulator	调压器
Primary Lock Reinforcement	加压型一次锁定
PRNDL	换挡照明灯
progressive air flow control	编程计算控制空气流量
prototype build	样品建造
Prototype Center	原型制造中心
puddle lights	泥水灯
pulse width modulation	脉宽调制(模型处理)
pump-handle primary lock	油枪锁
purge solenoids	清洗脱附电磁阀
push-to-seat	推入定位

Q

Quality	质量
Quiet Mini-Wedge latches Mini-Wedge	消音车门锁

R

rack and pinion	齿轮齿条式(转向机)
radiator	散热器
radio data system	无线电数据系统
radio mounting compartment	收音机安装仓
ramp	斜槽式
rapid age testing	快速老化测试
rapid prototyping technologies	快速样机设计技术
RDS	无线电数据系统
real-time dampers	实时缓冲器

real-time damping controller	实时减震控制器
real-time vehicle data acquisition	实时车辆数据采集
rear detection sensor	后探测传感器
rear-facing child restraint	婴儿座椅面向后保护
rear-facing infant seat detection	婴儿座椅面向后监测
rear fan	后风扇
rear radar	后视雷达
rear-steer-by-wire	电子伺服后轮转向控制
rebound and jounce damping capability	回弹和颠簸减振能力
receiver dehydrator	接液干燥器
recessed driver side module	凹陷式驾驶侧模块
recliner	侧斜靠背
reflector optics	聚光灯罩
refrigerant flow	冷媒(制冷剂流)
regenerative braking	再生制动
reinforced end wall	加强型端面壁
relative position sensor	相对位置传感器
remote displacement reservoir	远距排汽缸
remote keyless actuation	遥控门锁
remote keyless entry device	远距免用钥匙开车门装置
remote keyless entry	遥控电子钥匙
retainer piece	固定组件
retractable headlamp	伸缩式前照灯
returnless (mechanical) sequential fuel rail	无回路(机械)顺序燃油导轨
Rf remote control	频率遥控装置
ride and handling system	行驶和操纵系统
ride development engineering-driver-selectable	行驶开发工程设计——驾驶员任选(减振水平)
ride frequency	行驶频率
ride travel	行驶路程
road holding	着地性
roadside-to-vehicle information	路边与汽车间通信
rocker	摇架灯
roll	侧倾
roll bar	横摇稳定杆
roll control	侧倾摇控制
roll-by-wire	电子伺服侧倾控制
roller vane fuel pump	滚子叶片油泵

rolling code	滚动代码
rollover sensing	翻车感测
rotary switch	转盘开关
routed wire circuit bussing technology	定线式母线电气中心专利技术
routed wire technology	定线技术
routed wire	定线线路
routing plate	布线板
RTD damper	实时减振器
reppa joint	球笼式等速万向节

S

safety auto disconnect	安全自动断离
satellite	卫星天线
scroll	涡形管
sculpted vehicle interior	汽车内饰的雕镶格调
seal retention	密封保持
sealed/shielded brush holder	密封/屏蔽碳刷座
seals and gaskets	密封件和密封垫
seat adjusters	座椅调节器
seat belt locators	座椅安全带扣照明灯
seat deployment	座椅配置
seat position sensors and weight pads	座椅位置感测器和称重垫
seat positioning sensing	座椅位置感测
seat restraint	座椅固定位置
seat trim	座椅饰件
seat belt bulked sensing	安全带使用感测
secondary lock capabilities	二次锁定功能
secondary tools	辅助工具
segmented bus blade	分段母线片
self-adjusting and single-motion rod clips	可自我调节的单动式连杆夹
self-aligning head restraint	自对中头部保护装置
self-aligning blind mate connection	盲配合自对中连接
self-aligning head restraint	对中头部保护装置
self-lubricating silicone	自润滑硅材料
semi-active	半主动功能
semi-anechoic	半吸音
separator envelopes	袋式隔板
sequence in-line supply (SILS)	顺序交货方式
serrated crimps	锯齿形压接

service industry	售后服务
service tool	服务工具
sheet vinyl	乙烯树脂护板
shelf life	存放寿命
shield	护罩
shielded	带护罩
Shock Absorbers-Monotube, Twintube, Airlift-air meters	减振器-单管,双管,空气举升-空气计量器
shroud	屏板
shroud connector	护套连接器
side airbag modules and control electronics	侧面安全气囊模块及控制电子装置
side detection sensor	侧面监测传感器
side detection system	侧面监测系统
side impact countermeasures	车侧冲击缓冲件
side window defogger grilles	侧面车窗化霜格栅
side-impact collision	侧面撞击
side marker	宽度标志灯
sidewall trim	车身侧面饰板
signal-level sensors	信号电平传感器
silicone key cap	硅胶键罩
silicone overmold	硅胶面塑技术
sill button locking	车门窗栏按钮锁定
Simplified Chinese translation of "Delphi Terms"	德尔福专业术语简体汉字版本
single connection assembly	一体式连接组件
single front of dash passthrough	前挡板连接单一通道
single point responsibility	专人负责(一条龙服务)
single point source	专人对口负责
single row	单列
single source supply	专人负责供货服务
single-feed power distribution	单线馈电动力分配
single-feed grounding	单点定位
sleeve	套管
slip ring assembly	滑环组件
smart airbag	"智能型"安全气囊
smart car	智能汽车
smart parts	智能部件
smooth road feel	平顺的路感
snap fit airbag modules	卡扣式安全气囊模件

snap-fit components	卡扣固定元件
snap-in column	卡扣式转向柱
snap-in driver side module	卡扣式驾驶侧模块
snap-in magnesium steering column	卡扣式镁质转向柱
snap-on design	卡扣式设计
snap-on steering wheel	卡扣式转向盘
soft keys	弹性键
soft touch/soft feel control button	软触/柔感控制按钮
software-controlled wire routing process	软件控制定线工艺
solder	锡焊方式;焊接方式
solenoid valve and pressure switch	电磁阀和压力开关
solenoid	电磁开关
sounder	报警器
spark delivery	火花发送
spark energy	火花能源
spark plug wires	火花塞电缆
speaker grilles	喇叭格栅
special low corroding positive grid	特种低饰正栅极
speed and position sensors	速度及位置传感器
spin-sealed no-leak terminals	旋转密封方楼端子
splash protection	防溅保护
splash shield	防溅挡板
splash/corrosion	溅污及腐蚀
splice	分接
Splice Saver connectors Splice Saver	连接器
splicing altogether	电线胶缠
spline shaft	花键轴
split brake system	前后式制动系统
split leather	拼合皮革
sport-utility	多用途运动车
Sports Utility Vehicle (SUV)	多功能越野车
sporty handling	越野型驾驶
sprayed urethane	喷塑聚氨酯
spring member	弹簧形式
stabilizer bar control system	平衡杆控制系统
stabilization algorithm	稳定算法语言系统
stabilizer bar	稳定杆
stamped metal	冲压金属板

stamped serrations	冲压细齿
standard and adjustable steering columns	标准及可调式转向柱
Standard Terminal Cavity	标准端子插孔
state-of-the-art prototyping	现代化样机制作
static and dynamic test	静态和动态测试
static deployment station	静态配置站
steering angle sensor	转向角度传感器
steering column	转向柱
steering column attachment	方向柱固定器
steering gear	转向机
steering system	转向系统
steering wheel insert	转向盘骨架
steering wheel mounted controls	转向盘面控制元件
stereolithography	激光塑造工艺
stopping distance	制动距离
storage bin	储藏箱
straight ratio	不变传动比
strain relief	张力释放
streamlined	流线型
stress deformation analysis	压力变形分析
striker	碰锁机构
stripping cable	剥开电缆
structural urethane foam	结构聚氨酯(SRIM)
struts	支柱
strut	柱式减振器
Super Plug**TM door hardware module system	Super Plug**TM 车门五金模件系统
Super Plug**TM module	Super Plug**TM 模件
supplemental inflatable restraint system	辅助充气式乘员保护装置
surface and solid modeling wire frame	平面和立体线条模型
surge tank	稳压罐
surge tanks	膨胀水箱
suspension bushings	悬架衬套
suspension geometry	悬架几何结构
suspension yoke	铝质悬架轭
suspension	悬架
switch backlighting	开关背向灯
System Optimization	系统优化

Systems and Modules	系统和模块
T	
tangless	非缠绕系列
tangless terminal	无凸舌端子设计
Technological Leadership	技术领先
technology portfolio	技术多元组合
telematics	远距传送系统
television	电视频道
terminal engage	端子咬合力
terminal position assurance	端子定位组件
terminal retention force	端子保持力
terminal to terminal engage forces	端子至端子咬合力
terminating cable	割断电缆
text-to-speech	文字-话音切换
the illuminated entry system (IES)	车门入口照明系统
the power of advanced thinking	超前思维的动力
the power to simplify	于简化中见实力
theft-deterrent system	防盗预警
thermal expansion valve	热膨胀阀
thermal management	热管理
thermal runaway failure	热脱落
thermal shock	热冲击
thermoplastic elastomer	热塑弹性材料
thermostatic expansion valve	恒温膨胀阀(TXV)
thin profile seating	薄形座椅
thin stock FE terminal	细桩(FE)端子
three dimensionally shaped piece	三维形状的整体椅套
three-way valve, open-center, rotary-type	三位旋转阀(中心开放)
throttle body	节气门体
throttle body injection	单点式(节气阀体)喷射系统
throttle cable	节气门连接缆
throttle position sensor	节气门位置传感器
throttle-by-wire	电子伺服节气门控制
thru-the-partition extrusion fusion welds	接片及全腔挤出熔接技术
thrust	冲击力
tie bars/brackets	悬架连接杆/支架
tie rod	(免维修)拉杆
Tier II supplier	二级供货商

timing and exhaust gas recirculation	正时和废气再循环率
tin plated	镀锡
toggle switch	扳钮开关
top load installation	高载荷安装
torque sensing steering	转矩感应转向
torsion bar	转矩杆
total chassis systems	完整底盘系统
total system approach	整体系统方法
total vehicle thermal management system (TMS)	汽车全面热管理系统
tower connector	塔形连接器
to age an converter 10,000 miles	将催化转换器老化成为相当于行驶了10000英里（约合16093.4千米）之后的时效部件
TPA	端子定位组件
TPA with Primary Connector Lock	带连接器一次锁定的端子定位组件
traction	牵引力
traction control system	牵引力控制系统
traffic message channel	交通信息频道
transmission oil	变速器油
transmission shift control	变速器挡位控制
transmission shift solenoid	变速杆电磁线圈
transmission solenoid coil	变速器电磁线圈
transponder	转发器
transverse	横向
trim attachments	车内装饰固定件
trim line	汽车内饰装配线
trim plates	装饰板
trip computer	车载路程计算机
triple-rib peripheral seals	三肋周边密封
tripot joint	三销式万向节
tube and fin	管片交换式
tube and fin design	管片式
tunable pedal feel	可调节板力感
tuners	调谐器
turning radius	转弯半径
twilight sentinel	弱光感测
two- and four-corner leveling	两角或四角调平功能

two-corner rear leveling system	两角后调平系统
two-piece terminal design	两件结合式多路连接终端
two-rib cable seals	两肋电缆密封
two-shot cover	双层盖
TXV	热力膨胀阀
typical application	典型应用

U

U-channel	U 型流
ultrasonic interior protection system	超声波车内保护系统
under-the-hood	车盖下电子装置
underbody light	车梁灯
Unigraphics solid modeling	Unigraphics 实心模型制作
unwanted electrolyte loss	电解液不应有的消耗
upper control arm	（铝质）高位控制臂
upper instrument panel pads (topper pad with a full carrier)	上层仪表盘底盘（带整个托架的上底盘）

V

vacuum booster	真空助力器
vacuum forming	真空成型
VAG	大众汽车集团
Valisys reliability assurance software	Valisys 可靠性保证软件
valve block assembly	阀块组件
valve lifter	气门挺杆
valve train	配气机构组系
valve train systems	气门机构系统，配气机构系统
valve trains	配气机构部件
variable bleed	可变漏泄处理
variable compressor	可变排量空压机
variable displacement	可变排量
variable effort steering systems	可变作用力转向系统
variable output airbag inflators	可变输出安全气囊充气泵
variable ratio	可变传动比
variable tortional rate	可变扭转率
variable valve actuation	可变气门执行机构（VVA）
vehicle and validation test	汽车整车试验和产品验证试验
vehicle body hardware concept	汽车车体硬件设计
vehicle data interface	汽车数据接口
vehicle immobilization	汽车防起动技术

vehicle information	汽车信息频道
vehicle integration	汽车整合
vehicle platform	汽车平台配套
vehicle roll control	控制汽车侧倾
vehicle stability enhancement system	汽车稳定性增强系统
vehicle to roadside communications (VRC) transponder	汽车与路边通信转发器
vehicle dynamics	汽车动态性能
Vision	展望(德尔福亚太区刊物)
voice command interface	话音指令接口
voltage retention	电压保持
volumetric efficiency	容积效率
volumetric efficiency	充气效率
VRLA	阀门调节式铅酸蓄电池

W

warranty rate	保修费用
washcoat	基层涂料
waste spark coils	废点火线圈
water blown foam	水压泡沫
water resistant	抗水型
water tank	水室
water-based paints	水基涂料
Weather Pack Connection System	Weather Pack(全天候)连接系统
wedge-shaped striker	楔形门眼
welded wire spokes and stamping	焊接钢线轮辐和冲压
welded wire spokes and tubular rim	焊接钢线轮辐和管状轮圈
wheel speed sensors	车轮转速传感器
wheel spindle bearings	轮轴轴承
wheelbase	轴距
window regulator	车窗升降器
windshield defroster grilles	挡风玻璃化霜格栅
wire dress cover	电线压平盖罩
wire harness	点路线束
wire shield	金属网护罩
wires/boots	电缆/护套
wiring harness	点路线束
wiring harness production environment	点路线束制造环境
wiring splices	电路铰接头

Wu Han Grand Motor Co.	武汉万通汽车公司
www	万维网

X

X-by-wire	电子伺服技术

Y

yaw rate sensor	横摆比率传感器
yaw	侧倾

Z

zero emission	零尾气排放
ZEV zone	零尾气排放区

附件3 汽车维修手册缩略语表

缩写	全文	译文
A		
ABM	Anti-lock Brake Module	防抱死制动模块
ABS	Antilock Brake System	防抱死制动系统
ACEA	Association des Constructeurs Europeens d'Automobiles	欧洲汽车制造协会
ACM	Airbag Control Module	安全气囊控制模块
ADHL	Automatic Dynamic Headlamp Leveling	自动动态前照灯高度调节
AECM	Airbag Electronic Control Module	气囊电控模块
ALR	Automatic Locking Retractor	自动锁紧安全带卷收器
AOSM	Airbag On/Off Switch Module	安全气囊 ON/OFF 开关指示灯模块
APM	Adjustable Pedal Module	踏板调整模块
APPS	Accelerator Pedal Position Sensor	加速踏板位置传感器
ASD	Automatic Shut Down	自动切断继电器
ASI	Advance Service Information	维修信息预报
ATC	Automatic Temperature Control	自动温度控制
ATDC	After Top Dead Center	上止点后
ATF	Automatic Transmission Fluid	自动变速器油
AWD	All Wheel Drive	全轮驱动
AWL	Airbag Warning Lamp	安全气囊报警灯
AZC	Automatic Zone Control	自动区域控制
AZCM	Automatic Zone Control Module	区域温度自动控制模块
B		
BAF	By Active Function	被激活功能

BAS	Brake Assist	辅助制动
BCM	Body Control Module	车身控制模块
BEM	Battery Engine Manager	蓄电池能量管理
BLD	Brake Limiting Differential	制动限压差系统
BPS	Barometric Pressure Sensor	大气压力传感器
BTS	Belt Tension Sensor	安全带张紧传感器
BTS	Battery Temperature Sensor	蓄电池温度传感器
BTSI	Brake/Transmission Shift Interlock	制动/变速器换挡互锁
BUE	Built-up for Export	用于出口车型

C

C/T	Compass/Thermometer	指南针/温度计
CAB	Controller Antilock Brake	防抱死制动控制器
CAN	Controller Area Network	控制器局域网
CCN	Cabin/Compartment Node	车厢隔板节点
CCV	Crankcase Ventilation	曲轴箱通风
CGM	Central Gateway Module	中央网关模块
CHM	Cabin Heater Module	电热塞模块
CHMSL	Center High Mounted Stop Lamp	中央高位制动灯
CKP	Crankshaft Position Sensor	曲轴位置传感器
CLM	Climate Module	气候模块
CMP	Camshaft Position Sensor	凸轮轴位置传感器
CMTC/CMT	Compass Mini-Trip Computer	指南针和微型旅程电脑
COP	Coil-On-Plug	一体式火花塞
CPS	Camshaft Position Sensor	凸轮轴位置传感器
CPS	Cycles Per Second	波长/秒
CRS	Coolant Recovery System	冷却液回收系统
CV	Constant Velocity (Joint)	等速(万向节)
CVS	Calculated Vehicle Speed	计算得到的车辆速度

D

DAA	Digital Audio Amplifier	数字式音响功率放大器
DAB	Driver Airbag	驾驶员侧安全气囊
DCA	DaimlerChrysler Academy	戴姆勒克莱斯勒学院
DCC	DaimlerChrysler Corporation	戴姆勒克莱斯勒公司
DDM	Drivers Door Module	驾驶员侧门模块
DEMM	Dual Element Microphone Module	双元麦克风模块
DHSS	Dual High Side Switch	双高压侧开关
DIS	Distributorless Ignition System	无分电器点火系统
DLC	Data Link Connector	数据通信连接器
DMM	Digital Multimeter	数字万用表
DOHC	Dual Overhead Camshaft	双顶置式凸轮轴
DRB Ⅲ	Diagnostic Scan Tool	诊断读数器
DRL	Daytime Running Lamp	日间行车灯
DSD	Driver Sliding Door	驾驶员侧滑动车门
DTC	Diagnostic Trouble Code	诊断故障码
DVOM	Digital Volt Ohm Meter	数字电压和电阻表

E

EATX	Electronic Automatic Transmission Controller	自动变速器控制器
EBD	Electronic Brake Distribution	电子制动分配
EBH	Electric Back Heater	电动后窗加热器
ECM	Engine Control Module	发动机控制模块
ECT	Engine Coolant Temperature	发动机冷却液温度
ECTS	Engine Coolant Temperature Sensor	发动机冷却液温度传感器
ECU	Electronic Control Unit	电子控制单元
EDR	Event Data Recorder	瞬间数据记录器
EGR	Exhaust Gas Recirculation	废气再循环
EHV	Electric Heating Ventilating	电加热和通风
ELR	Emergency Locking Retractor	紧急锁止式伸缩装置

EMCC	Electronically Modulated Converter Clutch	电子调制液力变矩器离合器
EMI	Electromagnetic Interference	电磁干扰
EMIC	Electro Mechanical Instrument Cluster	电子机械组合仪表
EOL	End of Line	线路端
EPA	Environmental Protection Agency	环保局
ESM	Electronic Shifter Module	电子换挡模块
ESN	Engine Serial Number	发动机系列号
ESP	Electronic Stability Program	电子稳定程序
ETC	Electronic Throttle Control	电子节气门控制
EVA	Electronic Vibration Analyzer	电子振动分析仪
EVBP	Electronic Variable Brake Proportioning	电子可变制动比例阀
EVIC/VIC	Electronic Vehicle Information Center	电子车辆信息中心
EWD	Electric Wiper Defogger	电动刮水器除霜器

F

FCM	Front Control Module	前控制模块
FMVSS	Federal Motor Vehicle Safety Standards	联邦汽车安全标准
FWD	Front Wheel Drive	前轮驱动

G

G	G-Force	重力
GCS	Global Claims System	全球索赔系统
Gen II	Second Generation	第二代
GPIB	General Purpose Interface Bus	通用接口总线
GWA	Global Warranty Administration	全球索赔管理

H

HCU	Hydraulic Control Unit	液压控制单元
HD	Heavy Duty	重载
HFM	Hands-Free Module	免提模块
HID	High Intensity Discharge	高强度放电器

HOAT	Hybrid Organic Additive Technology	有机混合添加剂技术
HSD	High-pressure Sliding Driver	高压侧驱动器
HSM	Heating Seat Module	加热座椅模块
HVAC	Heating Ventilating Air Conditioning	暖风空调

I

I/O	Input Output Device	输入输出设备
IAC	Idle Air Control	怠速空气控制
IAT	Intake Air Temperature Sensor	进气温度传感器
IC	Integrated Circuit	集成电路
ICU	Integrated Control Unit	集成控制装置
IKB	Inflatable Knee Blocker	充气式膝盖安全气囊
IOD	Ignition Off-Draw	点火开关断后电流消耗
IPM	Integration Powertrain Module	集成动力模块
ISIS	International Service Information System	国际维修信息系统

J

JB	Junction Box	接线盒
JTEC	Jeep/Truck Engine Controller	吉普/载货汽车发动机控制器

L

LCD	Liquid Crystal Display	液晶显示器
LD	Light Duty	轻载
LDP	Leak Detection Pump	泄漏监测泵
LED	Light Emitting Diode	发光二极管
LEV	Low Emission Vehicle	低排放车辆
LFD	Lateral Force Deviation	横向力偏差
LFV	Lateral Force Variation	横向力变化
LHD	Left Hand Drive	左置转向盘
LID	Location Identifier	位置标志
LIN	Local Interconnect Network	局域网络

LOC	Loss of Communication	信号损失
LRSM	Light and Rain Sensor Module	光和雨传感器模块
LSA	Left Side Airbags	左侧安全气囊
LSD	Low-pressure Sliding Driver	低压侧驱动器
LSIAC	Linear Solenoid Idle Air Control Valve	线性怠速空气控制阀
LTFT	Long Term Fuel Trim	长期燃油修正

M

MAP	Manifold Absolute Pressure Sensor	进气歧管绝对压力传感器
MDS	Mopar Diagnoistic System	Mopar 诊断系统
MDS2@	Mopar Diagnostic System-2nd Generation	Mopar 第二代诊断系统
MHSM	Memory Heated Seat and Mirror	座椅和后视镜记忆模块
MIC	Mechanical Instrument Cluster	机械组合仪表
MLS	Multi-Layer Steel	多层钢片
MMT	Methylcyclopentadienyl Manganese Tricarbonyl	甲基环戊二烯三羰基锰（一种汽车燃油添加剂）
MSM	Memory Seat Module	座椅记忆模块
MTBE	Methyl Tertiary Butyl Ether	甲基叔丁基醚
MTC	Manual Temperature Control	手动温度控制
MTV	Manifold Tuning Valve	进气歧管翻转阀
MUX	Multiplexed	电阻式多路开关
MY	Model Year	年度型

N

NAE	North American California Emission	加州排放标准
NAFTA	North American Free Trade Area	北美自由贸易区
NAG1	New Automatic Gearbox 1st Generation	新型自动变速器第一代
NC	Normally Closed (switchstate)	常闭
NGC	Next Generation Controller	下一代控制器
NHTSA	National Highway Traffic Safety Administration	国家高速公路交通安全管理局

NO	Normally Open (switchstate)	常开
NTC	Negative Temperature Coefficient	负温度系数
NVH	Noise Vibration and Harness	噪声、振动和 悬架不舒适度
NVLD	Natural Vacuum Leak Detection	自然真空泄漏检测
NVM	Non-Volatile Memory	永久性存储器

O

OBD	On Board Diagnostics	车载诊断
OCM	Occupant Classification Module	乘员分类模块
OCS	Occupant Classification System	乘员分类系统
ODO	Odometer	里程表
OEM	Original Equipment Manufacturer	原始设备制造商
ORC	Occupant Restraint Controller	乘员安全控制器
OSHA	Occupational Safety and Health Administration	职业安全与健康管理局
OTS	Overhead Trip Information System	顶置旅程信息系统

P

P/N	Park/Neutral	驻车/空挡
PADL	Passenger Airbag Disable Lamp	乘客安全气囊失效指示灯
PCI	Programmable Communications Interface	可编程通信界面
PCM	Powertrain Control Module	动力控制模块
PCV	Positive Crankcase Ventilation Valve	曲轴箱通风阀
PDC	Power Distribution Center	配电中心
PDM	Passenger Door Module	乘客侧车门模块
PEP	Peripheral Expansion Port	外设扩展接口
PHS	Powertrain Hydraulic Steering	液压动力转向
PLGM/PLM	Power Liftgate Module	电动举升门模块
PLP	Principle Locating Position	主要定位点
PPS	Proportional Purge Solenoid	比例净化电磁阀
PSD	Passenger Sliding Door	乘客滑动门

PSDM	Passenger Sliding Door Module	成员侧电动滑动车门模块
PTC	Positive Temperature Coefficient	正温度系数
PTU	Power Transfer Unit	功率传输元件
PWM	Pulse Width Modulated	脉宽调制

Q

QHSS	Quad High Side Switch	方形高压侧开关

R

RAM	Random Access Memory	随机存储器
RD	Relay Drive	继电器驱动器
RFI	Radio Frequency Interference	无线电干扰
RFIS	Rear Facing Infant Seat	朝后的婴儿座椅
RFV	Radial Force Variation	径向力变化
RHD	Right Hand Drive	右置转向盘
RKE	Remote Keyless Entry	遥控无钥匙进入系统
RPS	Rollover Protection System	翻车保护系统
RSA	Right Side Airbags	右侧安全气囊
RSM	Rain Sensor Module	雨量传感器模块
RTV	Room Temperature Vulcanizing	常温固化胶
RWD	Rear Wheels Drive	后轮驱动

S

SAB	Side Airbag	侧安全气囊
SABIC	Side Airbag Inflatable Curtains	车门侧帘式充气安全气囊
SAC	Side Airbag of Curtain	车门侧帘式安全气囊
SAE	Society of Automotive Engineers	汽车工程师协会
SAS	Satellite Acceleration Sensor	加速踏板位置传感器
SB	Service Bulletin	维修公告
SBEC	Single Board Engine Controller	单板发动机控制器
SBT	Serial Bus Transmission	串行总线传输

SC	Speed Control	速度控制
SCCM	Steering Column Control Module	转向管柱控制模块
SCI	Serial Communication Interface Bus	串行通信接口总线
SCM	Steering Column Module	转向管柱模块
SCTM	Safety Belt Control Time Module	安全带计时控制模块
SDAR	Satellite Digital Audio Receiver	卫星数字音频接收器
SIACM	Side Impact Airbag Control Modular	侧撞安全气囊控制模块
SKIM	Sentry Key Immobilizer Module	安全钥匙防盗模块
SKIS	Sentry Key Immobilizer System	安全钥匙防盗控制系统
SKRES	Sentry Key Remote Entry System	安全钥匙遥控系统
SLA	Short Arm/Long Arm	不等长悬架
SLA	Shift Lever Assembly	换挡杆总成
SNA	Signal Not Available	无信号
SOHC	Single Overhead Camshaft	单顶置式凸轮轴
SPS	Speed Proportional Steering	速度比例转向
SRS	Supplemental Restraint System	辅助的乘员安全系统
SRTV	Short Runner Tuning Valve	短气道转换阀
SSV	Solenoid Switching Valve	电磁开关阀
STFT	Short Term Fuel Trim	短期燃油修正
STPS	Seat Track Position Sensor	座椅导轨位置传感器
STS	Special Tests	特殊测试

T

TCC	Torque Converter Clutch	变扭器离合器
TCCM	Transfer Case Control Module	分动器控制模块
TCCS	Torque Converter Clutch Solenoid	变扭器离合器电磁阀
TCM	Transmission Control Module	变速器控制模块
TCS	Traction Control System	牵引力控制系统
TDC	Top Dead Center	上止点
TDR	Transmission Data Recorder	变速箱数据记录器

TFT	Thin Film Transistor	薄膜晶体管
TFV	Tractive Force Variation	牵引力变化
TIPM	Totally Integrated Power Module	动力集成模块
T-MAP	Throttle MAP(calculated MAP value)	计算的 MAP 数值
TOT	Transmission Oil Temperature	变速器油温
TPM	Tire Pressure Monitor	轮胎压力监测器
TPS	Throttle Position Sensor	节气门位置传感器
TRS	Transmission Range Sensor	变速器挡位传感器
TSB	Technical Service Bulletin	技术维修公告
TTS	Transmission Temperature Sensor	变速器温度传感器

V

VES	Video Entertainment System	视频娱乐系统
VFD	Vacuum Fluorescent Display	真空荧光显示器
VIN	Vehicle Identification Number	车辆识别代码
VOV	Variable Orifice Valve	变孔径阀
VSS	Vehicle Speed Signal	车速信号
VTSS	Vehicle Theft Security System	汽车防盗系统

W

WCM	Wireless Control Module	无线控制模块
WOT	Wide Open Throttle	节气门全开
WSS	Wheel Speed Sensor	轮速传感器

参 考 文 献

[1] 陈家瑞.汽车构造[M].5版.北京:人民交通出版社,2006.
[2] 林平.汽车发动机机械系统检修[M].北京:人民交通出版社,2011.
[3] 许炳照.汽车底盘机械系统检修[M].3版.北京:人民交通出版社股份有限公司,2019.
[4] 张宗荣.汽车电气系统检修[M].北京:人民交通出版社股份有限公司,2015.